HD 9696 .1  W9-BMJ-068

Zeil, Deone.

Changing by Design

Changing
by DESIGN

Organizational Innovation at
HEWLETT-PACKARD

Deone Zell

ILR Press/an imprint of Cornell University Press

Ithaca and London

First published 1997 by Cornell University Press.

Library of Congress Cataloging-in-Publication Data

Zell, Deone.
    Changing by design : organizational innovation at Hewlett-Packard
/ Deone Zell.
      p.   cm.
    Includes bibliographical references and index.
    ISBN 0-8014-3298-7 (cloth : alk. paper)
    1. Hewlett-Packard Company—Management.   2. Electronic industries—
United States—Management—Case studies.   3. Organizational change—
United States—Case studies.   I. Title.
HD9696.A3U655   1997
338.7′61004165—dc21   96-46708

Printed in the United States of America

♲ This book is printed on Lyons Falls Turin Book, a paper that is totally
   chlorine-free and acid-free.

Cloth printing   10 9 8 7 6 5 4 3 2 1

To my mother,
for her love and support

CONTENTS

List of Figures   viii

Acknowledgments   ix

PART 1: A New Economic Landscape

1 Introduction   3

2 The Rise and Fall of Mass Production   7

3 New Business Principles and Practices   13

4 Strategies for Change   19

PART 2: Work Redesign at Hewlett-Packard

5 The Setting and Research Methods   35

6 The Roseville Surface Mount Center Redesign   49

7 The Santa Clara Division Redesign   87

PART 3: Changing by Design

8 Redesigning Organizations as Systems   135

9 Harnessing Human Potential   141

References   163

Index   173

FIGURES

1. Sociotechnical system principles 27

2. HP values and objectives 37

3. Roseville Surface Mount Center production relationship map 57

4. Organizational design: Bull's-Eye model 62

5. Roseville's Bull's-Eye model 63

6. Santa Clara Division organizational chart, before and after redesign 93

7. Santa Clara Division values 95

8. Santa Clara Division new product development process map 100

9. Santa Clara Division Bull's-Eye model 138

ACKNOWLEDGMENTS

This book would not have been possible without the inspiration and support of many people. First I thank the Sloan Foundation, especially Hirsch Cohen, as well as Gerald Geismar and the California Employment Training Panel, which provided generous financial support for research. I also thank the members of the California Worksite Research Committee, especially Benson Munger and Marvin Brodie, for their wisdom and guidance. Much gratitude also goes to the UCLA professors who provided intellectual challenge and growth: Joel Fadem, John Hawkins, William Ouchi, Hans Schollhammer, and the late Leigh Burstein. I am especially grateful to Harold Levine, who taught me how to be a participant-observer, and to Buzz Wilms for his encouragement and support. Much appreciation also goes to Dennis Cuneo and Bill Childs from NUMMI and to Bill Haley from USS-Posco, who turned auto plants and steel mills into places of learning. I also thank Scott Burton, Peter Gaarn, Mary Nur, Stu Winby, Vivian Wright, and Sharon Zimmerman from Hewlett-Packard's Change Management Team for sharing cutting-edge thinking and insights into the process of organizational change. Thanks also to my UCLA research team, Alan Hardcastle, Karen Ramsey, and Sergio Sotello, with whom I shared long, exhilarating hours inside factories and debriefings. My sincerest gratitude goes to Jenny Brandemuehl, Kathy Hendrickson, and Marty Neil of Hewlett-Packard, who were wonderful teachers. I also want to thank, at the Roseville Surface Mount Center, J. D. Brown, Dennis Early, Bob Hamilton, Steve Hibbert, John Hunter, Irene Kater, Matt Lee, Steve Perry, Randy Sharp, Dave Struthers, and Steve Tracy. At Santa Clara, I am especially grateful to Mark Allen, Matthew Bigham, David Chu, Dave Dills, Keith Ferguson, Bruce Greenwood, Lyle Hornback, Jim Johnson, George Lutz, Jerry Purmal, Errol Shanklin, Bob Shultz, Murli Thirumale, and Bob

Wilson. Finally other people who provided inspiration in important ways are Alexander Astin, Lena Astin, Andrea Goodwin, James Goodwin, Lucy Hesky, Susie Mais, Ted Mitchell, Richard Moore, Yvonne Moore, Deborah Rosenbaum, Nicky Squires, Greg Steiger, Mia Steiger, Dorothea Stokker, and Johanne Zell.

D. Z.

1 • A NEW ECONOMIC LANDSCAPE

1 • INTRODUCTION

We are witnessing a remarkable transformation of the American industrial landscape as companies are being forced to adapt to a rapidly changing and unpredictable global economy. An increasing number of firms are recognizing that they must shed the rigid, hierarchical organizational structures that supported mass production and replace them with flat and flexible structures to enable them to respond quickly to changing customer demands. Companies that succeed are also realizing that they must replace the underlying assumptions and beliefs that rationalized routine production work and sharply delimited employee participation in decision making with new and inclusive ones. Companies that can make this transformation find that their employees' capacity to learn provides a powerful competitive advantage. No longer can employees be treated like so many interchangeable parts. Rather, employees and managers, from the shop floor to the executive suites, must be aligned in a common mission, and they must be equipped with the skills, knowledge, and authority necessary to make fast decisions to respond to the changing environment.

But making such a transformation is difficult. Companies that founder often do so for two reasons. First, some executives fail to perceive their organizations as systems and try to bring about comprehensive change through only partial or fragmented efforts. For instance, some might introduce incentive systems such as profit sharing to improve productivity, while others might add quality circles to capture employees' suggestions for better product quality. But such piecemeal efforts fail to acknowledge the interdependencies that exist between organizations' structures and technology and their people. Second, managers, conditioned by the belief that it is their sole responsibility to make decisions, frequently find it extremely difficult to share their traditional authority with employees, even though such sharing is now becoming a requirement.

This book is about one large and very successful company—Hewlett-Packard (HP)—and how its managers are rediscovering a set of principles

3

that were invented over fifty years ago to avoid these pitfalls. It is a de-tailed ethnographic account of how managers of two HP divisions tapped their employees' know-how to redesign their organizations so they could successfully compete in the new economic order. This firsthand account reveals how including employees in every step of redesigning an organiza-tion results in a powerful form of learning, one that builds the necessary employee capacity and commitment to transform an organization suc-cessfully. These principles, embodied in a change strategy called "socio-technical systems redesign," or "organizational redesign," have been qui-etly used in companies for decades but the strategy has remained in relative obscurity because it requires radical change and is hard to do.[1] Today, however, the principles that underlie organizational redesign are experiencing a renaissance as the uncertainty and pace of change increases, compelling companies toward radical action if they are to survive.

Part I (Chapters 2, 3, and 4) is intended to broaden readers' under-standing of organizational change and to provide a historical context for the case studies. Chapter 2 summarizes the dramatic rise and fall of mass production which once led America to economic preeminence but today is a liability in the face of intense competition and an unpredictable environ-ment. Chapter 3 describes the emergence of mass customization, a new business concept that sets new standards for employee involvement and flexibility. Chapter 4 reviews two popular strategies for change—Total Quality Management (TQM) and Business Process Reengineering—and explains why neither is able to produce the necessary knowledge and com-mitment to respond quickly to changing conditions. Also in Chapter 4, I introduce the concept of organizational redesign, a strategy that engages employees in designing their own work systems to produce organizations that can learn from their environment.

Part II (Chapters 5, 6, and 7) gives the reader an insider's view of orga-nizational redesign at Hewlett-Packard to see how it actually works. Chap-ter 5 introduces the giant electronics company and describes the research method I used to capture HP's work redesign efforts in rich detail. Chap-ters 6 and 7 show how managers and employees in the two HP divisions struggled to share power, expand their thinking, and learn new behav-iors—efforts that produced handsome rewards.

Part III (Chapters 8 and 9) draws on learning from each of the cases to show how redesigning organizations as systems and investing in em-ployees' capacity to learn are now business imperatives. Chapter 8 ex-plains the importance of conceptualizing organizations as interrelated

---

1. Throughout this book, I will refer to sociotechnical systems (STS) redesign as organiza-tional redesign, or just redesign.

parts and spells out the requirement to align employees, technology, and organizational structure in the service of a common vision. Chapter 9 explains the process of harnessing human potential by translating learning into a sustainable competitive advantage and underscores the need for employees to become partners in organizational change.

My hope is that this book may help managers and leaders faced with similar challenges to engage their employees' talents so their organizations may survive and prosper. These detailed case studies, and the findings they produce, may also help all students of organizational change better to understand organizations as integrated wholes and the requirement that employees play leadership roles in any transformational efforts.

2 • THE RISE AND FALL OF MASS PRODUCTION

Modern organizations' work systems, structures, and cultures are reflections of the mass production system that emerged almost a century ago and led the United States to economic preeminence. Mass production was the next logical step after craft production, which had been the dominant mode of production well into the nineteenth century; products were made one at a time by artisans who used hand tools to turn raw materials into finished goods. Craft production was an art form, and the goods it produced were priced beyond the reach of most of society. It was also unable to keep up with the demands of a growing and expanding twentieth-century America which required vast quantities of food, agricultural implements, and industrial tools.

Mass production came to life in America with the automobile. To make the assembly of his 1908 Model T more efficient, Henry Ford discovered how to standardize parts and make them interchangeable so that workers no longer had to file down each part to fit. Rather, they could simply add standard parts that were machined to fit and bolt them into place. The hallmark of mass production, however, was Ford's moving assembly line. By bringing each car to a stationary worker, the moving assembly line eliminated the amount of time needed for workers to walk from car to car (Womack, Jones, and Roos, 1990). It was a tremendous innovation. When Ford introduced the moving assembly line to produce the 1913 Model T, the amount of labor time required to make a single car dropped from twelve hours and eight minutes to two hours and thirty-five minutes. Six months later, Model Ts rolled off the assembly line at a rate of one thousand a day, and the average labor time dropped even further to just over ninety minutes (Chandler, 1977). By 1916, the Ford Motor Company had manufactured over five hundred thousand cars. Ford's huge economies of scale dropped the unit price from $850 to $360, making the Model T affordable for most American families (Hounshell, 1984).

Ford perfected not only the interchangeable part but also the interchangeable worker. Workers in his Highland Park, Michigan, plant spoke more than fifty different languages, and many spoke little English. Yet they were able to produce the Model T because Ford had taken the division of labor to the extreme by organizing jobs to eliminate the need for cooperation. Before 1913, skilled fitters were responsible for a range of tasks. Each gathered all the necessary parts, obtained tools from the tool room, assembled the entire vehicle, and checked his work before sending the completed automobile to the shipping department. In contrast, assemblers on Ford's mass-production line had only one task, for example, to put two nuts on two bolts or to attach one wheel to each car as it moved by. It was irrelevant that assemblers might not speak the same language because they had no need to talk to each other (Womack, Jones, and Roos, 1990).

The advance of mass production was accelerated by the writings of Frederick Winslow Taylor, who started out as a shop foreman at Philadelphia's Midvale Steel Company. Taylor, who pioneered scientific management, was an efficiency expert and maintained that reducing the movement associated with any given task would also reduce workers' fatigue, thereby increasing production and lowering costs. Guided by the belief that workers would become more effective if they concentrated on single tasks, he divided complex jobs into many different narrow and specific duties (Taylor, 1967). Taylor also advocated the separation of "thinking" work from its execution so that workers could function efficiently as extensions of their machines. "All possible brain work should be removed from the shop and centered in the planning or laying-out department," he wrote (1919:98–99). Managers would be responsible for gathering the knowledge that in the past had been possessed by workmen and then reducing this knowledge to rules, laws, and formulas. Finally, Taylor explained, "The work of every workman is fully planned out by the management at least one day in advance, and each man receives in most cases complete written instructions, describing in detail the task which he is to accomplish, as well as the means to be used in doing the work. . . . This task specifies not only what is to be done, but how it is to be done and the exact time allowed for doing it." (1967:39).

The principles of scientific management that rationalized mass production eventually gave rise to the early twentieth-century hierarchical organizations and came to pervade all sectors of American industry. In the automobile industry, for example, the roles of manager and engineer were created to control workers' movements by designing their work and planning their jobs in minute detail. With such a separation of mental and manual labor, workers required only a few minutes of training before they could be placed on the assembly line. Ford knew that it was unreasonable to expect workers to volunteer information about ways to improve operating conditions. That was the responsibility of the foreman and industrial engineers, who reported their findings and suggestions to higher levels of management (Womack, Jones, and Roos, 1990).

By the early 1950s, evidence of the assembly line's deleterious effects began to emerge. Several studies, most notably one by Charles R. Walker and Robert H. Guest, reported how workers complained about the monotony of their jobs and the incessant pace of the assembly line (Walker and Guest, 1952; Chinoy, 1955). By the 1960s and 1970s, worker dissatisfaction had become a national issue. Almost every major periodical in the United States featured articles on the "blue-collar blues" or "white-collar woes" (Braverman, 1975). A Special Task Force appointed by the secretary of Health, Education, and Welfare prepared an authoritative report called *Work in America* that found that "significant numbers of American workers are dissatisfied with the quality of their working lives." Dissatisfaction, the report said, translated into poor productivity: "As a result, the productivity of the worker is low—as measured by absenteeism, turnover rates, wildcat strikes, sabotage, poor-quality products, and a reluctance by workers to commit themselves to their work tasks" (Special Task Force, 1973:xvi–xvii).

Worker dissatisfaction and poor productivity were not limited to the assembly line or even to the factory. The Special Task Force also described similar trends in office environments: "The auto industry is the *locus classicus* of dissatisfying work; the assembly line, its quintessential embodiment. But what is striking is the extent to which the dissatisfaction of the assembly line and blue-collar worker is mirrored in white-collar and even managerial positions. The office today, where work is segmented and authoritarian, is often a factory. . . . Secretaries, clerks, and bureaucrats were once grateful for having been spared the dehumanization of the factory. White-collar jobs were rare; they had a higher status than blue-collar jobs. But today the clerk, and not the operative on the assembly line, is the typical American worker, and such positions offer little in the way of prestige" (Special Task Force, 1973:38–40).

Despite its adverse effects, the system of mass production was immensely successful and it helped drive the United States to economic preeminence. Assembly line work paid well, and unionized factory jobs were stepping-stones to the middle class. From the end of World War II to the early 1970s, the U.S. economy grew so rapidly that the standard of living doubled in a single generation (Johnson, 1994). Post–World War II American consumers had higher levels of discretionary income than those in any other nation, and they enjoyed unprecedented purchasing power. With available domestic markets eight times larger than those of any competitor, American companies could achieve huge economies of scale—and huge profits. The United States claimed the top scientists and the best managers in the world, and its technology was second to none. As the post–World War II American educational system proliferated, it produced generations of workers, managers, and technicians to support the system of mass production. Together, such vast internal markets, superior technology, huge amounts of capital, a well-educated labor force, and effective managers led the country to unprecedented economic success (Dertouzos et al., 1989).

But this success caused American industrial and labor leaders to become complacent and blind to the ominous changes that were taking place around them. By the early 1980s, Japanese electronics and automobile manufacturers began to penetrate deeply into American markets. In just a few years, American manufacturers had lost huge segments of their automobile, steel, electronics, and semiconductor markets. For instance, by 1987, about two-thirds of all foreign cars imported into the United States were Japanese (Dertouzos et al., 1989). Similar patterns were evident in other industries. By 1986, Japanese steel imports had risen to 37 percent of domestic consumption. By the late 1980s, American electronics manufacturers had lost 95 percent of their domestic market to the Japanese. Similarly, the American semiconductor industry that once commanded 60 percent of the world market had shrunk to 40 percent by the late 1980s, while Japan's share had almost doubled, from 28 to 50 percent. By 1991, Japanese imports were responsible for three-quarters of America's $43 billion trade deficit with Japan (Dertouzos et al., 1989; Schoenberger, 1992).

Today, however, the U.S. automobile, steel, and semiconductor industries have achieved a remarkable comeback, although merely catching up with international competitors is not enough to ensure continued prosperity because the rest of the world has also improved just as quickly. There is little doubt that uncertainty and rapid change will continue to characterize the international economy for at least three reasons:

Competition: The emergence of the global market has increased the intensity of competition to levels never imagined. Following in Japan's footsteps, the "little tigers"—Taiwan, South Korea, Hong Kong, and Singapore—have emerged as manufacturing giants and quickly taken over the international consumer electronics industry. Competition continues to intensify as formerly undeveloped countries such as Indonesia, India, and China are now exporting a growing number of products to the United States (Thurow, 1995b).

In addition to an increase in the absolute number of competitors, the nature of competition itself has changed. As historic trade barriers have fallen and the transportation and communications industries have become modernized, products and services can be created and sold anywhere, and no company is immune to overseas competition (Thurow, 1995a). For instance, Caterpillar competes with Komatsu of Japan in heavy moving equipment, DuPont competes with Hoechst of Germany in the chemical industry, and Chase Manhattan Bank competes with Barclays Bank in the United Kingdom. The point is that when producers from different countries are free to compete in the same world market, one superior performer automatically raises the competitive standards for the rest.

Technology: A second factor that has raised competition is the proliferation of increasingly sophisticated process technology that helps to design and manufacture new products and speed their delivery to market. For example, in research and development (R&D), computer-aided design and computer-aided manufacturing enable engineers to create images of cars and computers in virtual reality, check the assembly of their parts, and evaluate their ergonomics without ever actually producing a real product. On the factory floor, computer numerical control, direct numerical control, and industrial robots greatly increase manufacturing flexibility by controlling the manufacture of parts through software programming. In addition, flexible manufacturing systems ensure that all members of a family of parts can be manufactured at will and at random, meaning there are no cost penalties for manufacturing one part instead of another. Finally, computer-integrated manufacturing links these "islands of automation" into a single integrated system that is fast and flexible and produces high volumes at low cost (Spira and Pine, 1993).

Such superior process technology is a major reason for Japan's success, and it promises to give Japan a competitive advantage well into the twenty-first century. Though conventional wisdom once held that *product* technology produced higher rates of return than investments in *process* technology, Japan has shown that the opposite can be true. For instance, about 70 percent of Japanese R&D capital investments are made in new processes, while only 30 percent goes into new product development. In the United States, the pattern is reversed. Only 30 percent of R&D capital is invested in new process development, while 70 percent goes into new product development (Thurow, 1995a). As a result, three leading products, the video recorder and camera and the fax invented by Americans and the CD player invented by Europeans, have become Japanese products. The point is that simply being able to *invent* products is no longer a competitive advantage. There is little doubt that as the capabilities of computers, software, and telecommunications continue to develop at exponential rates, the rate of technological change will continue to increase as well (Thurow, 1995a).

Customers: Third, customer preferences have changed profoundly. In the years following World War II, mass producers built standardized products for a relatively homogeneous market. Although the American market was not truly homogeneous, consumers bought standardized products because they had no choice. Despite their lack of options, American customers were relatively satisfied because nothing better was available.

But today, with such a vast number of competitors who produce wide varieties of high-quality, low-cost products, customers have virtually unlimited choices. Manufacturers are differentiating their products further by providing high-quality service. For instance, Japanese customers can custom-design their own car in a dealer's showroom and be assured that the product will be manufactured, tested, and delivered to their doorstep within five days (Pine, 1993).

With so many options available, customers' expectations have soared. Many no longer accept standardized products, while others demand to be treated individually with products and services configured to their unique needs. In short, today's customers know what they want, how much they want to pay for it, and when they want it. These customers have few incentives to deal with companies that fail to grasp this new buyer-customer relationship (Hammer and Champy, 1993).

3 • NEW BUSINESS
PRINCIPLES AND PRACTICES

Such intense competition, proliferating technology, and a dramatic rise in customers' expectations have forced many companies to acknowledge that mass production is no longer adequate. In its place new concepts such as "flexible manufacturing," "time-based competition," and "rapid response" are emerging, all of which can be grouped under a new label called "mass customization."[1] The concept of mass customization was first anticipated in 1970 by Alvin Toffler in his book *Future Shock*, but the term was actually coined in 1987 by Stan Davis in his book *Future Perfect*. The idea has gained fresh currency in a recent book, *Mass Customization*, by Joseph Pine II, an IBM manager (1993).

The goal of mass customization is to deliver high-quality, low-cost products tailored to the needs and tastes of individual customers (Dertouzos et al., 1989; Davidson and Davis, 1990). Mass production aimed to minimize costs and maximize volume by standardizing products, whereas mass customization aims to provide variety and customization through a flexible and responsive production process. Aided by new process technologies such as flexible manufacturing systems and computer-integrated manufacturing techniques, mass customization shortens product development cycles and offers a continuous stream of high-quality, low-cost goods and services tailored to niche markets. Taken to its extreme, mass customization would actually produce lot sizes of one, each of which would be custom-designed for individual buyers (Pine, 1993).

Some industries have already adopted the principles of mass customization. For instance, auto buyers can now choose from over two hundred different car models with a large number of options that can be combined in seemingly infinite ways—from stereo systems that provide the acoustics

1. Mass customization is also known as agile production, or agile manufacturing. See John H. Sheridan, "Agile manufacturing: Stepping beyond lean production," *Industry Week* 242 (April 19, 1993):30–46.

of a jazz club, to suspension systems that enable riders to choose between "soft" and "sport" rides (Pine, 1993:35–36). Toyota offers customers the ability to design customized cars on computer-aided design systems in dealer showrooms or even in their own homes. Orders are processed, cars are scheduled for production, and are manufactured, tested, and delivered in five days (Goldhar, Jelinck, and Schlie, 1991).

The principle has spread to other industries as well. For instance, only a short time ago, telecommunications services and products were standardized with options ranging between pulse or rotary telephones or WATS (wide area transmission service). Following deregulation in 1984, the competition has produced a staggering array of options. Customers can choose call forwarding, call waiting, caller identification, caller ID blocking, multiple phone lines each with a different ring, and voice "mailboxes." The fast-food industry has also adopted mass customization. Until recently, McDonald's successfully mass produced billions of high-quality burgers and french fries. Today, however, its menu has expanded to include pizza, chicken fajitas, breakfast burritos, spaghetti and meatballs, carrot and celery sticks, and even bottled mineral water (Scarpa, 1991).

The implications of these innovations are becoming clear. Companies that compete in industries characterized by rapid technological change and diverse product markets must become more nimble and responsive to remain competitive. Providing customers with such variety and responsiveness requires tremendous flexibility in production systems as well as in employees, who are closest to customers and who are becoming increasingly important (Kanter, 1993). Orders for customized products must go straight to self-managing teams of employees on the shop floor who have the authority to make quick decisions about production planning, schedules, and forecasts. Such teams can rapidly bring together their skills, knowledge, and experience to respond to sudden, unpredictable changes in the environment (Pine, 1993). Shifting responsibility for decision making to the shop floor, however, will require that organizations dismantle their hierarchical, bureaucratic structures, shed their "command and control" cultures, and decentralize power (Beer and Walton, 1990; Sheridan, 1993). Organizations' business processes must be reengineered to eliminate waste and to reduce cycle times. Finally, employees must be motivated to help their organizations transform and be compensated for their increased commitment and their expanded roles as they take on greater responsibility for decisions and for the organization's business success. In short, shifting from an organization built around mass production to one that is flexible and able to respond to a changing environment will require fundamental changes in these new organizations' structures, work systems, and human resource practices.

The most critical ingredient for succeeding with these new businesses will be a skilled and committed workforce. In his newest book, *The Post-Capitalist Society*, Peter Drucker argues that in the new economy, the knowledge worker is the single greatest asset, and an organization's most essential resource is "qualified, knowledgeable, dedicated people" (1993: 56). Economist Lester Thurow (1992:51) explains that "while technology creates man-made comparative advantage, seizing that man-made comparative advantage requires a work force skilled from top to bottom. The skills of the labor force are going to be the key competitive weapon in the twenty-first century. Brainpower will create new technologies, but skilled labor will be the arms and legs that allow one to employ—to be the low-cost masters of—the new product and process technologies that are being generated." Unless employees are given greater breadth in their jobs and more responsibility and are able to understand and control a larger part of the production process, say the authors of *Made in America,* the full advantages of new technologies like flexible, computer-aided manufacturing systems cannot be exploited (Dertouzos et al., 1989).

Many of the proposals for expanding workers' roles and responsibilities have already been the subject of much discussion. For instance, Frederick Herzberg's job enrichment plans in the 1950s and the Quality of Work Life (QWL) movement in the 1960s and 1970s, which sought to make jobs more varied and interesting and increase workers' participation, were used by managers to raise workers' morale, improve their attitudes, and avoid unionization. These efforts, however, were intended to affect a company's performance only indirectly (Appelbaum and Batt, 1994). In these years, American companies were riding mass production's wave of success, and few executives saw any economic reason for employees to have a broader range of skills. In fact, such workplace "innovations" as job enlargement and team-based systems were declared "frills" by most managers, and they could be cut back at any time to reduce costs. Only since the 1980s have companies begun to recognize participative decision making as part of their competitive strategy rather than as a tactical tool for improving job satisfaction (Appelbaum and Batt, 1994).

OBSTACLES TO CHANGE

Making the transition from a hierarchical, bureaucratic organization to a flat, flexible one, however, is exceedingly difficult, and many efforts fail for reasons mentioned earlier and discussed below in detail (Walton, 1975; Lawler, 1991).

Failure to View the Organization as a System

Organizations are complex systems composed of interrelated parts that must constantly readjust to respond to the environment (Katz and Kahn, 1978; Beer, 1980). Lacking this conception of organizations as systems, many managers believe they can transform their companies in a piecemeal fashion, implementing limited changes in some parts of their organizations but failing to redesign the organization as a whole. For example, managers might create quality circles, set up self-managing teams, implement gain-sharing programs, or reengineer work processes, but not recognize that each change requires supporting changes in others. As the authors of *Made in America* explain, "Managers today often acknowledge that one or another feature of [the mass production] model ought to be scrapped, and so, for example, they will set up quality circles or reduce batch sizes. But everything we have learned from our industry studies in the United States and abroad suggests that individual parts of the old patterns cannot be replaced piecemeal. . . . Rather, for any of the reforms to survive and flourish, the environment in which it is implanted must be transformed" (Dertouzos et al., 1989:49).

It is not that techniques like reengineering, Total Quality Management, or self-managing teams are inherently bad. Rather, they tend to be partial rather than comprehensive strategies for change (Kilman, 1995; Kling, 1995). When any of these techniques are implemented in isolation and necessary supporting changes are not made in other parts of an organization, their effect will be limited at best. For example, trying to implement self-managing teams without altering an organization's authoritarian culture will fail. Or reengineering a business process without at the same time obtaining the support of managers and employees responsible for running the process will produce resistance rather than commitment to the change. Not only is it common sense, but it has been demonstrated empirically that fragmented changes are far less effective than systemwide efforts (Ichniowski, Shaw, and Prennushi, 1993; Laabs, 1993; Macy, Izumi, Bliese, and Norton, 1993). For example, follow-up studies at General Electric found that none of its hundred self-managing work groups survived because no concomitant changes were made in the roles of managers, and support personnel were not changed in ways to support the team structure. At AT&T, a large-scale effort to provide telephone operators with more decision making met with only limited success because the layers of management were not reduced, preventing authority from moving downward (Lawler, 1991). Because organizational changes are mutually reinforcing, they must be considered and implemented together rather than as independent solutions from which managers can pick and choose (Dertouzos et al., 1989; Davidson and Davis, 1990).

Nevertheless, in the face of this evidence, companies continue to implement changes in a disjointed fashion and to get only marginal results. After a review of 185 case studies of workplace change, Eileen Appelbaum and Rosemary Batt (1994) concluded that "U.S. companies have largely implemented innovations on a piecemeal basis and that most experiments do not add up to a coherent alternative to mass production" (1994:10). But systemwide efforts at change are rare because they are hard to do and they carry higher risks than changing one piece of an organization at a time. As the authors of *Made in America* note, "Implementing such far-reaching innovations involves wrenching changes at all levels of the organization and requires an extraordinary commitment by corporate leaders" (Dertouzos et al., 1989:126).

Shedding the Culture of Mass Production

A related problem is how to replace the underlying culture—the beliefs and assumptions that grew out of mass production—with new beliefs to guide organizations in this new and unpredictable environment. The primary obstacle to diffusing the best industrial practices, according to the MIT Commission on Industrial Productivity, was the "continuing influence of ways of thinking and operating that grew out of a mass-production model" (Dertouzos et al., 1989:49). Although many executives advocate reducing layers in their organizations and diffusing authority downward, few have put these ideas into practice. The number of companies that report using self-managing teams to involve workers in day-to-day decisions is growing, but most efforts are limited to small subsets of workers (Lawler et al., 1995). Most efforts to decentralize authority take the form of "parallel structures" such as quality circles and problem-solving teams— strategies that allow managers to draw on employees' knowledge about how to cut costs or how to make work processes more efficient while retaining control over decision making. These strategies may improve quality and employees' motivation, but they rarely result in fundamental changes in the way work is done (Appelbaum and Batt, 1994).

Shifting authority and responsibility downward requires a change in the basic assumptions that guide the assignment of tasks and responsibilities by encouraging and supporting participation, teamwork, and decision making at lower levels of the organization (Zager and Roscow, 1982:xiv). But this also requires altering an organization's power structure, which is exceedingly difficult because managers find it very hard to give up control (Beer and Eisenstat, 1996). As a result, "sharing power, authority, responsibility, and decision making is uncharted territory for most U.S. managers, and many are reluctant to cede power to workers on and off the shop floor" (Appelbaum and Batt, 1994:151). Similarly, participatory work structures such as self-managing teams often fail to survive because the "demands that they make simply require more change than many managers are willing to voluntarily accept" (Lawler, 1991:118). As a result, despite the popularity of "empowering" employees, most organizations resist this fundamental change and instead retain the hierarchical, bureaucratic structures and the underlying cultures that were so successful under mass production.

4 • STRATEGIES FOR CHANGE

TWO of the most common strategies to improve organizational performance that have received widespread attention are Total Quality Management and Business Process Reengineering. Both are examples of techniques that, for different reasons, often fail to produce the desired results because they do not sufficiently alter organizations' structures, cultures, and work processes and thus fail to produce an overall transformation. What they have in common—a "top-down" approach to change—limits their abilities to alter an organization's power structure and to obtain the knowledge and commitment among employees that are necessary to respond quickly to changing conditions (Schaffer, 1988; Beer, Eisenstat, and Spector, 1990).

TOTAL QUALITY MANAGEMENT

Total Quality Management emphasizes continuous quality improvement and customer satisfaction by incrementally improving an organization's work processes. TQM is based on the assumption that the cost of quality (e.g., costs of developing processes that produce high-quality products and services) is far less than the cost of poor workmanship (inspection, rework, lost customers) (Hackman and Wageman, 1995). Work processes are improved through the use of a systematic set of tools and practices that include statistical process control and quality improvement teams (Mohrman et al., 1995). Because of TQM's focus on incremental improvement, however, managers have found it inadequate to produce fundamental change in an organization's work processes or in its performance. As we shall see, TQM's top-down style of implementation makes it impossible fundamentally to alter organizations' centralized power structures.

TQM grew out of America's recognition that Japan's success in making high-quality products stemmed from its use of employee problem-solving groups called quality circles. Attempts to recreate quality circles in American firms failed largely because American workers were less motivated to help managers improve quality than were their Japanese counterparts. This realization led American managers to recognize that obtaining the full benefits of statistical process control would require more than setting up groups and training them in statistical process control—it would require a new philosophy of management that encouraged employees to help improve quality (Mohrman et al., 1995). Eventually, the TQM philosophy became widespread through the work of W. Edwards Deming, Joseph Juran, and Kaoru Ishikawa, who today are considered icons of the TQM movement.

TQM prescribes five main practices. First, companies must get explicit knowledge about their customers' requirements and focus quality improvement on the appropriate work processes. Second, suppliers should be chosen on the basis of their product quality rather than solely on product price. Third, companies should use teams to identify and solve quality problems that usually span more than single functions. Fourth, TQM requires the use of scientific methods and statistical tools (e.g., control charts, Pareto analysis, and cost-of-quality analysis) so that managers and employees can analyze and monitor their work processes. Fifth, process-management tools should be used to enhance team effectiveness. Three of the most commonly used devices are flow charts, brainstorming, and cause-and-effect diagrams, or "fishbone" diagrams (Hackman and Wageman, 1995).

TQM is typically implemented and driven by top management out of the conviction that quality is ultimately its responsibility. Senior managers reason that because they themselves create the organizations, any quality-improvement process must begin with their own commitment to total quality (Hackman and Wageman, 1995). TQM programs typically begin by training top managers in the philosophy of quality, followed by articulating and communicating a "quality vision" (Conference Board, 1991). Both education about TQM and its implementation are expected to cascade downward through an organization with each level carrying the message to the next lower level.

TQM enjoyed strong and steady growth until the early 1990s, when its popularity appears to have leveled off. According to a 1993 survey of Fortune 1,000 companies, 76 percent that responded reported that they had a TQM initiative in place, up only slightly from 73 percent in 1990. TQM has drawn national attention partly by recognizing companies that have exemplary quality programs with a prestigious award called the Malcolm Baldrige National Quality Award, named after Malcolm Baldrige, a former secretary of commerce (Lawler et al., 1995).

Although most firms report supporting TQM initiatives, only a few of the practices advocated by Deming, Juran, and Ishikawa are actually in widespread use. According to the Fortune 1,000 survey, the two most common practices were improvement teams and monitoring customer satisfaction. Only 35 to 40 percent of the companies, however, reported using self-inspection, collaboration with suppliers, and directly exposing employees to customers (Mohrman et al., 1995; Lawler, Mohrman, and Ledford, 1995).

The popularity of TQM probably derives in part from its ability to adapt to an existing hierarchy (Lawler, 1994). One problem with TQM is that although it advocates employee involvement, it retains centralized decision making and does little to alter an organization's power structure. As a result, there is an inherent limit to the degree to which TQM can fully empower employees without threatening managerial control (Hackman and Wageman, 1995). Employee involvement was never explicitly recommended by TQM's founders but became associated with TQM because it was interpreted as a necessary step toward improving an organization's work processes (Haley, 1985; Deming, 1986). Not surprisingly, employee involvement is typically limited to workers who participate in problem-solving committees and quality circles that are directed by first-line supervisors or higher-level managers (Appelbaum and Batt, 1994).

A second problem with TQM is its inability to bring about fundamental change in an organization's core work processes. Many studies make the point that TQM is not an appropriate strategy for companies that require a radical organizational change (Chorn, 1991; Teng, Groven, and Fiedler, 1994). J. Richard Hackman and Ruth Wageman (1995) assert that TQM leans toward only modest interventions and contributes little to changing how front-line work is structured or to how authority is distributed. In other words, while TQM can help fine-tune companies' existing business processes, it cannot fundamentally alter the mass manufacturing system of production. In effect, TQM aspires to "achieve fundamental change without changing the fundamentals" (Hackman and Wageman, 1995:319).[1]

BUSINESS PROCESS REENGINEERING

In the early 1990s, companies witnessed the phenomenal rise of a new and revolutionary approach to performance improvement called Business Process Reengineering. Reengineering is formally defined as "the funda-

---

1. For a thorough discussion of the implementation of TQM at Douglas Aircraft see Alan Hardcastle's doctoral dissertation, "The voices of organizational culture: An ethnographic study of total quality management implementation at Douglas Aircraft Company" (Ph.D. diss., University of California at Los Angeles, 1994).

mental rethinking and radical redesign of business processes to achieve dramatic improvements in critical, contemporary measures of performance, such as cost, quality, service, and speed" (Hammer and Champy, 1993:32). The widespread popularity of reengineering reflected managers' judgment that TQM and other such strategies were not dramatic enough to improve performance and were inadequate to deal with new demands for flexibility (Lathin, 1995). Put another way, incremental improvement was insufficient to meet changing customer expectations (Macdonald, 1995). Companies needed methods that would lead to change that was revolutionary, not evolutionary.

Many executives initially regarded reengineering as the perfect solution because it was so radical. In their book, *Reengineering the Corporation,* Michael Hammer and James Champy explain that reengineering means "tossing aside old systems and starting over" and should be used only when an organization is in need of "heavy blasting" (1993:31, 33). Reengineering, the authors say, is an "all-or-none" proposition that produces dramatically impressive results—not 10 or 20 percent improvements but "quantum leaps in performance" (5, 33). Reengineering seeks "breakthroughs" not by enhancing existing processes but by discarding and replacing them with entirely new ones (49). Traditional organizations, they explain, are organized like functional silos, or "stovepipes"—vertical structures built on narrow pieces of a process such as R&D, finance, and manufacturing. Reengineering aims to redefine organizations around critical crosscutting (horizontal) processes such as product development, procurement, and order fulfillment.

Reengineering also appealed to American managers because of its top-down philosophy. Hammer and Champy make no apologies: "It is axiomatic that reengineering never, ever happens from the bottom up" (1993: 207). Front-line employees and middle managers, they say, cannot be expected to implement a successful reengineering effort because they lack the broad perspective that reengineering demands and do not understand how all the process activities fit together. In a typical reengineering project, a small group designs work processes for a larger group. As a result, there is little participation in the design process by those who actually do the work (Davenport, 1995b).

By 1994, reengineering had taken management by storm. Nearly two million copies of Hammer and Champy's *Reengineering the Corporation* had been printed in English (Womack, 1995). Some surveys show that as many as 88 percent of large corporations claim to do Business Process Reengineering and many others plan to begin soon (Bashien, Markus, and Riley, 1994). Reengineering has now been tried by two-thirds of American companies and most of those in Europe (*Economist*, 1995). U.S. firms paid consultants $7 billion in 1994 to help them reengineer their companies (Womack, 1995).

But by 1995, the bad news began to surface, showing that reengineering efforts had failure rates as high as 70 percent (Hall, Rosenthal, and Wade, 1993; *Economist*, 1995; *Harvard Business Review*, 1995). According to one widely quoted estimate, 85 percent of reengineering projects fail (Womack, 1995). Thus, despite its initial promise, by 1995 reengineering's popularity had faded (Micklethwait and Wooldridge, 1996).

Part of reengineering's downfall was its association with layoffs. Although Hammer and Champy argued vigorously that reengineering was not synonymous with restructuring or downsizing, it was often used to trim companies' payrolls quickly. This fact was documented by the CSC Index, the management consulting firm that pioneered reengineering, in its 1994 "State of Reengineering Report." According to the report, nearly three-quarters (73 percent) of all companies surveyed said they were using reengineering to eliminate jobs (Davenport, 1995a).

A more serious drawback to reengineering is that it overlooks the human side of organizational change. By separating the design of work from its execution, reengineering repeats the same error in human judgment that was inherent in Taylorism. Small design teams of high-level managers and process engineers apply rational tools to reach a decision on the "best" way to organize work. But employees play no role in its creation, and they often reject the new design. By ignoring employees, reengineering fails to develop a sense of ownership and commitment to the change process among employees. One of the originators of reengineering, Thomas Davenport, admits that "reengineering treated the people inside companies as if they were just so many bits and bytes, interchangeable parts to be re-engineered" (1995a:71).

By the mid-1990s, critics began calling for "holistic" reforms that aimed at long-term growth rather than short-term gain (Flamholtz, 1995). Articles began to appear that emphasized the "soft" side of reengineering and stressed the critical role of employees in organizational restructuring (Galliers and Baker, 1995). According to an article in the *Economist*, some companies are now "reengineering with love" by asking workers to forsake their jobs for several months to do their own reengineering (1995:69). Chrisopher Bartlett, a professor at the Harvard Business School, and Sumantra Ghoshal, a professor at the London Business School, explain:

After the slash-and-burn organizational restructuring of the past decade, one thing is becoming increasingly clear to managers: if a company is to proceed beyond the shrinking spiral of downsizing and rationalization to develop the ability of continuous self-renewal, its real battle lies not in reorienting the strategy, restructuring the organization, or revamping the systems, but in changing individual organization members' behaviors and actions. A self-renewing organization can be built only on the bedrock of people who are willing to take personal initiative and to cooperate with one another, who have self-confidence and a commitment to the company, and who are able to execute relatively routine tasks with the same proficiency as they are willing to learn new skills and ways to take the company to the next stages if its ambition. In short, the most vital requirement for revitalizing businesses is to rejuvenate people. (1995:20)

Gradually, managers and scholars are recognizing that the human element must be restored to reengineering if it is to succeed, and they are realizing that employees themselves should be involved in the reengineering process. For example, two business professors write: "Increasingly, it is becoming clear that the engine of reengineering is not reengineering analysts, but managers and the people who do the work. Reengineering requires committed, empowered people, not simply to operate processes after they have been reengineered, but also to reengineer them in the first place" (Cooper and Markus, 1995:43). Today Davenport recommends "participative makeovers" of business processes instead of reengineering that has failed. He suggests taking a "middle of the ground" approach, rather than top-down or bottom-up, that allows for some direction from the top while acknowledging that business processes are essentially human processes. Such an approach would combine the reengineering discipline with employees participating in designing their own work.

Most observers have come to recognize that reengineering needs to be replaced with a process that acknowledges both the human and technical sides of an organization and one that relies heavily on the knowledge and participation of employees. Davenport acknowledges, "This is not a new idea. In the literature on socio-technical systems design, researchers recognized decades ago that participating in the design of work increased people's level of commitment to the new approach. . . . Unfortunately, this crucial concept has been largely ignored in the reengineering movement" (1995b:27).

SOCIOTECHNICAL SYSTEMS (STS) REDESIGN

Davenport is correct. STS redesign—a set of principles that aim to balance the human and the technical sides of an organization by having employees redesign their own work—is not a new idea. Rather, these principles have been quietly in use for nearly a half-century. The theory behind them emerged from efforts to improve productivity in English coal mines in the late 1940s (Trist and Bamforth, 1951; Rice, 1958; Davis, 1957; Emery, 1959; Walton, 1972; Herbst, 1974; Trist, 1976). Shortly after World War II, Tavistock Institute psychologist Eric Trist and a group of colleagues were commissioned to study how to improve productivity, safety, and morale in the mines. New technology to mechanize work had been introduced to the mines to boost productivity, but it had the opposite effect. Coal miners who had historically worked in tightly knit, self-managing teams were assigned specialized jobs. They were stripped of the authority they had always taken for granted, which now shifted upward to supervisors who were charged with controlling their activities. As a result, productivity plummeted while absenteeism and the number of accidents rose. But Trist discovered that when workers tried to reach a rich coal seam where the new machinery could not reach, they spontaneously regrouped themselves into teams that shared all tasks. They worked autonomously, took responsibility for entire work cycles, and participated in decisions about their work arrangements. Not surprisingly, the miners' morale and productivity increased, while accidents and absenteeism decreased (Trist et al., 1963; Weisbord, 1987). This discovery eventually led Trist to advocate the use of "composite work groups," or teams whose members were cross-trained so that each team could be relatively autonomous and responsible for an entire task. Such groups, said Trist, avoided the conflicts between technical and social aspects of work that had been created by functional specialization (Trist et al., 1963).

Over the years, Trist was joined by others in formalizing STS theory, which rests on two main tenets. First, work comprises two interrelated systems, the technical and the social, and superior performance can be achieved only by jointly optimizing *both*. Second, an organization is an "open system," a concept adapted from biology (von Bertalanffy, 1950). This biological open-system perspective assumes that an organization is affected by larger environmental forces and must constantly respond to them to survive through a constant two-way exchange of information (Davis, 1979).

In the 1950s and 1960s, STS principles were further elaborated by Scandinavian researchers, who became influential in the team-based restructuring experiments in Norway and Sweden in the early 1960s. Swedish reorganizations in the early 1970s successfully used autonomous work groups to improve worker morale and productivity, which eventually led to the restructuring of work along these lines in firms such as Volvo and Saab.

Principles of STS Redesign

The goal of STS redesign is to produce an organization that can adapt and perform successfully in a rapidly changing, turbulent business environment. The principles behind STS redesign were first enumerated by Albert Cherns (1976, 1987), who was head of the Department of Social Sciences at Loughborough University and a member of the Council of Tavistock Institute (see Figure 1).

The Process of Redesign

The key feature that differentiates STS redesign from other top-down forms of organizational improvement (such as TQM or reengineering) is that employees help redesign their own work systems (Appelbaum and Batt, 1994). Although there are no formal or rigid guidelines to STS redesign aside from the principles articulated by Trist and others over the last fifty years, certain tools and methods have been developed to diagnose and restructure organizations as systems. Today, the most commonly used method is one developed in Norway by Fred Emery and later refined by UCLA professor Louis Davis (Sherwood, 1988; Hitchcock and Lord, 1992).

The first step is to obtain sponsorship for the effort from a high-level executive who serves as a "champion" and provides political leadership and resources for the design team. The champion buffers the new work system from interference, maintains communications with the rest of the organization, and shares the risk.

Next, a steering committee is formed to guide the project. The steering committee is usually made up of key managers (and union officials in unionized companies) who represent all stakeholders whose support is essential for the success of any new work system. The steering committee authorizes the formation of a design team and oversees its creation. The steering committee has the authority to approve or modify recommendations made by the design team. It also serves to protect the new work system, once implemented, from pressures to conform to old ways. Finally, like the champion, the steering committee maintains communications with the design team and with the remainder of the organization.

The third step is the formation of a design team that includes front-line employees who actually do the work that is being redesigned. The design team conducts a three-step analysis that consists of a business analysis of an organization's environment; a technical analysis of the systems of work; and a social analysis of an organization's policies and culture. In a business

1. *Compatibility.* The process of designing an organization must be compatible with the organization's objectives—or, in other words, the means should fit the ends. This means, for example, that an organization that is to be participative cannot be created by fiat.
2. *Minimal critical specifications.* In deciding how work is to be carried out, no more should be stated than is absolutely essential. While it may be necessary to be precise about what has to be done, it is rarely necessary to be precise about how it is to be done.
3. *Variance control.* Variances, if they cannot be eliminated, must be controlled as near to their point of origin as possible. (A variance is any unintended variation in the production process that affects critical performance outcomes such as quality, cost, reliability, responsiveness, or safety. Examples include variations in a product's raw materials or a machine failure.)
4. *Boundary location.* Boundaries should *not* be drawn so as to impede communication. Traditional organizations are organized by functions (engineers are placed with engineers, assemblers in assembly, and the like). Often this results in a situation in which, for instance, an engineer working on a particular product line is grouped with other engineers on the other side of a wall from the production line and evaluated by a supervisor who is unfamiliar with the product line.
5. *Information flow.* Information should be provided first to those who will need it to act on it. In other words, information about production reports, budget variances, defects, or customers' preferences should go to those who control the work systems that can respond. This is contrary to the typical situation, where information is distributed based on power and those who will be most affected are the last to know.
6. *Power and authority.* Those who need equipment, materials, or other resources to carry out their responsibilities should have access to them and authority to command them. In return, they accept responsibility for them and for their prudent and economical use.
7. *The muiltifunctional principle.* Organizations should possess people with more skills than are needed at any time, rather than more people than are needed who know how to do only one thing.
8. *Support congruence.* The systems of social support should be designed to reinforce the behaviors which the organizational struc-

Figure 1. Sociotechnical system principles

ture is designed to elicit. For example, if teamwork is desired, the reward systems should support team behaviors, not individual performance.

9. *Design and human values.* An objective of organizational design should be to provide a high quality of work. Six intrinsic factors make work satisfying: variety and challenge; elbow room for decision making; feedback and learning; mutual support and respect; wholeness and meaning; and room to grow and a positive future.

10. *Transitional organization.* The period of transition is more complex than either old or new. In other words, making the transition from a traditional organization to a new one is far more difficult than starting anew in a "greenfield." The design team can serve as a vehicle of transition from old values to new.

11. *Incompletion.* Although periods of stability are essential to enable people to cope with change, the present period of transition is really between one period of transition to another. Redesign is not a task of special design teams but an ongoing process that must become internalized in self-regulating teams that control production on a day-to-day basis.

Figure 1. Continued

analysis, the design team members identify an organization's mission and values, the customers' requirements, and business trends. A business analysis often includes benchmarking trips to other companies to identify best practices and compare an organization against its competitors. In a technical analysis, the design team analyzes the organization's structure, employees' roles, and the design of the individual jobs. The team also maps the flow of production, identifies disconnects between processes, and identifies combinations of tasks that make up coherent pieces of work. In a social analysis, the design team analyzes the organization's culture, as well as policies and practices that influence employees' behavior such as hiring practices, incentive systems, and training. Finally, design team members analyze their findings to develop a comprehensive proposal to help an organization achieve its business objectives through the best fit of its technical and social systems. Several designs may be created before a final design is chosen and implemented.

Consultants (from either inside or outside the organization) are often used to help guide the redesign effort by stimulating creative thinking, help the team work effectively as a group, and help the design team members through their analyses (Sherwood, 1988).

Use of STS Principles in North America

STS principles have been used to design new plants (or "greenfields") and to redesign existing ones. The earliest experiment to create a new plant was a 1968 design project at the Aluminum Company of Canada's (Alcan) continuous process ingot casting facility in Arvida, Quebec. Next, Procter & Gamble (P&G) opened a new plant designed around STS guidelines in Lima, Ohio, but little is known about what actually happened because the company considered its strategy proprietary and has refused to publish anything about it (Taylor and Felton, 1993). The most ambitious and highly publicized new-design plant was General Foods' Gaines dog food plant in Topeka, Kansas. Built in 1969, the plant became a model for American industry and gave significant impetus to the *Work in America* report published by the U.S. Department of Health, Education, and Welfare (Yorks and Whitsett, 1989). More widespread use of STS redesign, however, did not emerge until the 1980s (Miles and Rosenberg, 1982; Nora, Rogers, and Stramy, 1986; Walton, 1985).

In the 1980s, a renewed interest in STS principles began to emerge, and today an impressive list of companies have used the principles, including AT&T, General Foods, PPG Industries, Procter & Gamble, Shell Oil, Sherwin-Williams, TRW, Digital Equipment Enfield, H. J. Heinz, Rockwell, Tecktronix, Johnson and Johnson, General Motors, Mead, Inland Steel, Cummins Engine, and Volvo (Lawler, 1991; Taylor and Felton, 1993). According to one estimate, by 1991 at least forty large corporations had used STS principles to design at least one new plant (Walton, 1985).

The limited data on the effectiveness of these new plants indicate that they are far more productive than their traditional counterparts. For example, studies of the General Foods Topeka plant reported 92 percent fewer quality rejects and 40 percent lower production costs than those of a comparable, traditionally managed General Foods plant (Lawler, 1991; Pasmore and Sherwood, 1992). A new Sherwin-Williams plant reported 30 percent higher productivity, absenteeism rates 63 percent below average, and costs that were 45 percent lower than those in the rest of the company. A Volvo plant's assembly hours were reduced by 25 percent, and its unit costs averaged 15 percent of those in its sister plants. A new Shell plant's output was 35 percent higher than and its absenteeism half that of comparable plants. The quality of work life in each of these organizations also improved significantly, as did job satisfaction (Pasmore and Sherwood, 1992).

The positive results reported by the new-design plants led these and other companies to apply the same principles to redesign existing plants.

Today this list of companies includes Procter & Gamble, Shell, Volvo, Cummins Engine, Citibank, General Electric, Honeywell, Motorola, and TRW (Pasmore and Sherwood, 1992; Lawler, 1991).

Like new plants, redesigned plants also produce positive results. For instance, Citibank reported that after a 1970 redesign, revenues increased by 400 percent and expenses remained constant despite a 15 percent annual increase in costs. A 1987 redesign at AAC Insurance reduced claim-processing time by 75 percent and increased productivity by 20 percent. Similar positive results have been reported for companies such as Shenandoah Life Insurance, General Foods, and General Electric (Pasmore and Sherwood, 1992). A 1994 redesign at Honeywell Circuit Boards produced quality improvements that ranged from 82 to 99.5 percent, a reduction in scrap from 18 to 1.5 percent, a reduction in unit costs of 46 percent, a reduction in product lead times from thirteen weeks to fifteen days, and a 280 percent increase in productivity. A recent large-scale, longitudinal study of 131 organizations that had undergone some form of redesign reported that those companies that followed STS guidelines—especially those that implemented semiautonomous teams and supporting changes in the organization's policies and practices—exhibited significant improvements in financial performance (Macy, Izumi, Bliese, and Norton, 1993).

While both new designs and redesigns produce positive results, the success rates of new designs are much higher than those of redesigns (Lawler, 1991). The reasons are obvious. New plants, or greenfields, can start from scratch, whereas redesigning an existing organization requires altering the entrenched structures, processes, and cultures that grew up around mass production.

Work Redesign in Nonlinear Environments

For the past thirty years, most successful redesign efforts have been done in high-volume manufacturing environments, where converting inputs into outputs is routine, sequential, and highly predictable. In these environments, STS principles have been applied to identify and control variances in linear production systems. But these principles can apply to nonlinear processes like R&D, where the core conversion process is one of producing knowledge, and process is nonroutine and nonsequential (Purser, 1991). The first application of STS principles to engineering work began in 1982 (Taylor, Gustavson, and Carter, 1986). Application of the principles to nonlinear knowledge and professional work did not become widespread until the late 1980s (Pava, 1983; Purser and Pasmore, 1990; Pasmore and Gurley, 1991; Purser, 1991). Virtually no data exist on the results of these efforts, however.

Despite the evidence that redesign tends to produce positive results, including employees in redesigning their work remains "largely virgin territory; almost all firms have undertaken either participative quality programs, or top-down reengineering programs" (Davenport, 1993:9). As a result, virtually no empirical research exists on how redesign actually works in practice. This book provides an inside look at both linear and nonlinear redesign in one of America's leading companies, Hewlett-Packard.

2 • WORK REDESIGN AT HEWLETT-PACKARD

5 • THE SETTING AND RESEARCH METHODS

This chapter provides an overview of Hewlett-Packard, its use of STS principles, and an introduction to the two divisions that were sites for the study. This chapter also explains how I used ethnography as a research method to observe and document the inner workings of everyday life at HP, its underlying culture, and the redesign process.

HEWLETT-PACKARD

Hewlett-Packard was founded in 1939 by William Hewlett and David Packard, who had just graduated from Stanford University with degrees in electrical engineering. They built their first product in the garage of Packard's rented house in Palo Alto, which today is a California historic landmark designated as the birthplace of Silicon Valley. The product was an electronic test instrument known as an audio oscillator that improved upon existing audio oscillators in size, price, and performance. HP's first big customer was Walt Disney Studios, which purchased eight oscillators to develop and test an innovative sound system for the classic movie *Fantasia*. Over the next fifty years, Hewlett and Packard built the company into a giant designer and manufacturer of a wide range of products, including computer systems and peripherals, integrated instrument and computer systems, test and measuring instruments, hand-held calculators, medical electronic equipment, and instrumentation and systems for chemical analysis. In 1995, the company employed more than ninety-four thousand people in more than sixty divisions worldwide, produced more than eleven thousand different products, and generated $31.5 billion in revenue (Hewlett-Packard Company, 1995). HP's achievements have not gone unnoticed, and in 1995 it was voted the top corporate performer in America by *Forbes* (Linden and Upbin, 1996).

An important factor in the company's success is its decentralized structure that keeps it flexible despite its size. HP is a collection of more than sixty produce divisions that have worldwide responsibility for their product lines. Hewlett and Packard set up the divisions to encourage autonomy and creativity, to avoid bureaucracy, and to encourage problem solving at the lowest possible level. Many divisions are vertically integrated, with their own R&D, manufacturing, marketing, personnel, controllership, and quality-assurance functions, although these may be geographically dispersed. Divisions are purposely kept small, usually no more than fifteen hundred employees. New divisions are created when a product line becomes large enough to support continued growth from its profits. Divisions with related products are often linked together by a common strategy into groups that have their own field sales organizations, making it possible to offer fully integrated solutions to customers and to consolidate marketing efforts.

The HP Way

Much of HP's success is attributed to its corporate culture, known as the "HP Way" (Ouchi, 1981; Kotter and Heskett, 1992). In the early years of the company, Bill Hewlett and Dave Packard developed a management philosophy and a style of running a business that has been singled out as a model for American companies and has been called a "legacy to American business" for its uncommon virtues and egalitarian beliefs (Flanigan, 1996). The HP Way is passed on from one generation of employees to the next, not through a process of indoctrination but rather through selection and a subtle, gradual process of acculturation. As new employees are exposed to the behaviors practiced by their managers and their fellow employees, they gradually conform and adopt them as their own. The objectives that underlie HP's organizational culture were first written down in 1957 and have changed very little since. Today these objectives, and the values on which they are based, are summarized in a document called "The HP Way" and in a small brochure entitled "Corporate Objectives" (HP Way, 1980; Corporate Objectives, 1989) (see Figure 2).

Trust and respect for individuals: Packard writes in his memoir published just before his death in 1996: "From the beginning, Bill Hewlett and I have had a strong belief in people. We believe that people *want* to do a good job and that it is important for them to enjoy their work at Hewlett-Packard. . . . It has always been important to Bill and me to create an environment in which people have a chance to be their best, to recognize their potential, and to be recognized for their achievements" (1995:126–27).

High level of achievement and contribution: All employees, especially managers, are expected to go out of their way to meet customers' needs and to look continuously for new and better ways to do their work. HP is

Values
- Trust and respect for individuals
- High level of achievement and contribution
- Conducting business with uncompromising integrity
- Achieving common objectives through teamwork
- Flexibility and innovation

Objectives
- Profit
- Customers
- Fields of interest
- Growth
- Our people
- Management
- Citizenship

Figure 2. HP values and objectives

very selective in considering job candidates and places great emphasis on their ability to adapt and to fit within the HP culture.

Conducting business with uncompromising integrity: HP employees are expected to be open and honest in their dealings to earn the trust and loyalty of others and are expected to adhere to the highest standards of business ethics.

Achieving common objectives through teamwork: Teamwork both within and among HP's divisions is valued because it is considered the only way that the company can fulfill the expectations of its customers and shareholders. Packard explains: "It's imperative that there be a strong spirit of helpfulness and cooperation among all elements of the company and that this spirit be recognized and respected as a cornerstone of the HP Way" (1995:128).

Flexibility and innovation: This value is to be encouraged by a work environment that supports the diversity of people and ideas. The company strives to create clear objectives and to allow employees flexibility in working toward them. HP employees are expected continuously to upgrade their skills and to adapt to change. Packard writes, "People must take sufficient interest in their work to want to plan it, to propose new solutions to old problems, and to jump in when they have something to contribute" (1995:153).

The HP Way also includes seven company objectives, which are the means by which the core values are expressed.

Profit: HP considers profit to be a critical objective because only by generating profit can the company accomplish its other corporate objectives. Packard writes, "The profit we generate from our operations is the ultimate source of the funds we need to prosper and grow. It's the foundation of future opportunity and employment security" (1995:83–84).

Customers: The company strives to provide the highest possible quality products and services and the greatest possible value to its customers and to gain and hold their respect and loyalty.

Fields of interest: HP pledges to participate in those fields of interest that build both on its technology and its customer base and that enable the company to make a needed and profitable contribution.

Growth: This is to be limited only by the company's profit and its ability to develop and produce innovative products that satisfy real customer needs. HP considers continuous growth in sales and profits essential to maintain a position of strength and leadership in its fields and to attract and retain the best possible people.

Our people: The company helps its employees to share in its success by providing employment security based on employees' performance, ensuring a safe and pleasant work environment, recognizing employees' individual achievements, and helping them gain a sense of satisfaction and accomplishment from their work.

Management: Managers are to foster initiative and creativity by allowing individuals freedom in attaining well-defined objectives.

Citizenship: The company strives to honor its obligations to society by being an economic, intellectual, and social asset to each nation and each community in which it operates. The company pledges to make sure that communities in which they operate are better for its presence ("Corporate Objectives," 1989).

In practice, the HP Way translates into an open, trusting environment and an extremely pleasant place to work. There are no closed-door offices at HP. Even top executives work in open spaces separated only by low-rise partitions. Such a physical layout supports the company's "open-door" policy, which encourages employees to discuss personal and job-related issues with their managers. Employees are encouraged to go up the line to higher-level managers if they feel uncomfortable talking to their immediate supervisors. "Management by walking around" or MBWA, a practice taught in business schools, originated at HP. Managers are encouraged to spend a part of each day wandering through the organization, often without any specific purpose other than to see what is going on and to communicate with employees. The company also practices "management by objective," or MBO, which Packard describes as the "antithesis of management by control" (1995:153). Managers set broad goals, and employees are free to meet them in ways they deem best. The HP Way also encourages trust. I remember being shocked when I saw how employees left their bicycles unlocked and expensive equipment sitting in plain view on their desks even when they were not there. It was a pleasant feeling to be able to leave my laptop computer or my purse unattended on my desk without a second thought. HP employees call each other by their first names, no matter their rank or positions. For example, when the Santa Clara division manager walked through the division, employees would wave and say, "Hi Marty!" At first, I was surprised to hear employees talk affectionately about the founders as "Bill and Dave." Employees are encouraged to mix socially, and they often share outdoor interests such as mountain and rock climbing. This extension of relationships from work to their personal lives reflects the "family feeling" to which employees so often refer. Everyone is salaried, no one punches a time clock, and employees are able to work flexible hours. They can start their work day very early or as late as 9 A.M. and can leave after working a standard eight-hour shift. Employees are also well rewarded for their efforts. They are regarded as owners and share in HP's success through generous stock purchase plans and profit sharing, which ranges from just over 4 to almost 10 percent of employees' base salary (von Werssowetz and Beer, 1982; Packard, 1995).

The company also places a strong emphasis on providing employment security, though it has never been a stated policy. Hewlett and Packard decided at the outset that they did not want to be a "hire and fire" company. Packard writes, "Bill and I didn't want to operate that way. We wanted to be in business for the long haul, to have a company built around a stable and dedicated workforce" (1995:129). HP has never had a major layoff. In the 1970 recession it asked employees to take a 10 percent pay cut, but no one was fired (Linden and Upbin, 1996). In business downturns, employees who are no longer needed are transferred to other divisions that are growing. In the 1990s, when the company was forced to reduce its workforce, it did so through early retirements and a program of voluntary severance, which provided employees who were willing to leave with a generous financial package. The company has never had a union. Packard once told a group of HP managers, "I have tried to follow the basic policy that I have more reason to be interested in my employees than a union leader does. As soon as the employees think that one of these union people is going to be more interested and responsive to their needs than I am, then I think they should have a union!" (1974).

Although the HP Way is articulated with unusual clarity, HP employees choose simple ways to describe exactly what it is. One Santa Clara manager explained, "If you go into an airport in a foreign country, or to an HP office in South Africa, you find the same character. 'Can I get you a cup of coffee? Can I help you somehow?'" Another Santa Clara engineer echoed the sentiments of many other veterans when he defined the HP Way. He whispered, "It's a *family*. It's so simple. I've been here thirty-some years and I used to see Bill and Dave every day. Everyone was on a first-name basis, you were expected to do your job, and you knew exactly where you stood. It wasn't any different than the family at home."

Redesign at Hewlett-Packard

In the late 1980s, an internal HP corporate action research and consulting group known as the Factory of the Future began working with divisions that were interested in organizational redesign. The group was charged with improving the company's business performance by creating a better alignment between its employees, technology, and business strategy. Stu Winby, who headed the group, chose a sociotechnical system (STS) framework because he knew that STS principles were compatible with the HP Way. Winby also believed that redesign would help divisions become more adaptable and flexible so they could better compete in HP's turbulent business environment. Winby's group began redesign projects within several HP divisions. Initially, these projects focused on manufacturing but soon spread to R&D and other nonlinear work environments—and later throughout the company's entire value chain. These early experiments produced positive results; divisions reported improved productivity and quality and shorter new product development cycles (Zell, Levine, and Wilms, 1992). In 1992, the first redesign of an entire division was initiated at Santa Clara. Also by the close of 1992, more than twenty divisions had undergone work system redesign, resulting in significant returns on their investments and saving the company millions of dollars (S. Winby, personal communication, September 23, 1993).

In the years that followed, STS tools and principles became so embedded in divisions' change processes that the name "STS" is no longer used. As the principles spread throughout the company, they evolved into a increasingly pervasive and sophisticated approach to performance improvement. According to Winby, "Today, we're using concepts like complexity theory and strategic knowledge management. But if you dig deeply into these new technologies, like peeling back the layers of an onion, at their core is STS philosophy—a systems philosophy" (S. Winby, personal communication, October 4, 1996).

The Two Sites

This book is based on the STS redesign efforts that took place in two divisions of Hewlett-Packard.[1] The first was a redesign of the Surface

---

1. The study was part of a larger study of industrial restructuring in California's automobile, steel, aircraft, and electronics industries based at UCLA's Graduate School of Educa-

Mount Center within the manufacturing arm of the California Personal Computer Division that began in late 1990. The Surface Mount Center manufactured printed circuit boards for HP's line of personal computers. Like many other computer makes at the time, HP was struggling to clarify its strategy in the tumultuous personal computer industry. Part of the company's emerging strategy involved consolidating the manufacture of personal computers, and in early 1990 the Surface Mount Center was relocated from the division's headquarters in the Silicon Valley to HP's manufacturing facility in Roseville, California. The center employed two hundred people, 30 percent of whom were temporary workers. Although business was growing for the center, its costs remained uncompetitive. Later that year, the center began a redesign to reduce its production costs. Several months into the project, the center's managers learned of the possibility that the center could be further consolidated with another HP division in Grenoble, France. Roseville's management team continued the redesign in hopes that the center's improved performance would influence top managers' decision regarding the final location of the consolidation—which, they hoped, would be California.

The second was a redesign of the entire Santa Clara Division in Santa Clara, California. Established in 1961, the division is located on the site of a former apricot orchard. It is HP's second-oldest division and one of twenty-two divisions in the company's Test and Measurement Organization. For more than twenty years the division produced highly sophisticated test and measurement instruments. In the mid-1980s, however, Santa Clara's traditional customers began to disappear and the division's revenues plunged. By the early 1990s, the division's workforce had been reduced from sixteen hundred to six hundred employees. In 1992, a new division manager took over and initiated a division-wide, cross-functional work redesign effort to try to restore growth and profitability. The division had to be transformed from a supplier of general-purpose instruments to a supplier of customer-specific products. The project also required a fundamental shift in the division's culture from one that was inwardly focused and driven by technology to one that was outwardly focused and responsive to customers' needs.

---

tion and conducted under the auspices of the California Worksite Research Committee. I was the manager of the HP portion of the study. The UCLA research team included two professors and four graduate students, of which I was one. The origin and results of the larger study were published in Wellford Wilms's *Restoring Prosperity* (New York: Random House, 1996).

RESEARCH METHODS

The main research method I used was ethnography, a qualitative method that allows the researcher to participate in everyday events and provides an insight into an organization's culture, as well as an understanding of how it changes.[2]

The goal of ethnography is to capture a holistic understanding of human behavior within a specific context or culture (Dachler and Wilpert, 1978). Ethnography also provides an insider's view of life within an organization, which facilitates understanding of the meaning of actions or events under study (Wax, 1971). Ethnography produces "thick descriptions" that reveal multiple meanings and interpretations of events and the underlying culture that produces them (Geertz, 1973:7). Some researchers say that ethnography succeeds if it teaches readers how to behave appropriately in any cultural setting, whether it be among natives in New Guinea or engineers in a semiconductor plant (Bogdan and Biklen, 1982).

The best-known ethnographic technique is participant observation, a "naturalistic" research technique, which means that the topics or people of interest are studied in their natural environment rather than in a laboratory. As its name implies, participant observation requires a researcher to participate in daily activities and to observe employees as they go about their work. The participant-observer usually participates in peoples' daily lives for an extended period of time, watching what happens, listening to what is said, and asking lots of questions. Participant observation thus helps a researcher to understand an organization from the inside, as the participants do themselves—a perspective that is missing in most studies on organizational change.

Participant-observation research has been conducted in various organizational settings over the last fifty years by students from such academic disciplines as anthropology, social psychology, industrial sociology, and management. Within industrial settings, it has been used as a research tool in case studies and cross-site comparisons to examine industrial cultures and the social organization of work, usually in blue-collar occupations and industries (see Applebaum, 1981; Rohlen, 1974; Roy, 1952; Savage and Lombard, 1986; Whyte, 1961).

The use of participant-observation methods to study organizational culture has increased in recent years. Most organizational research is conducted through interviews or as controlled, quasi-experimental studies to

---

2. For some excellent works on organizational culture, see Edgar H. Schein, *Organizational Culture and Leadership* (San Francisco: Jossey-Bass, 1989); Chris Argyris and Donald A. Schon, *Organizational Learning* (Reading, Mass.: Addison-Wesley, 1978); and Benjamin Schneider, ed., *Organizational Climate and Culture* (San Francisco: Jossey-Bass, 1990).

investigate human behavior. Interviews are a powerful means to explore individuals' views in great depth, but they cannot determine whether how people say they behave is really how they actually behave, nor can they capture nonverbal actions and events. Survey research is often based on a priori assumptions and hypotheses that can blind the researcher to unexpected or little-understood events. Survey research is useful for confirming and validating patterns of behavior, but it is inadequate for discovering new phenomena. Nor can it chronicle and analyze how a change process unfolds, which is what I have aimed to do here.

This book is intended to provide a detailed account of the practical application of STS redesign principles. Most reports of redesigns are case studies that provide surface-level descriptions of how the effort was conducted, and they conclude with the results (see, for example, Sherwood, 1988; Reese, 1995; Auguston, 1989; Hogan, 1993; Rehder, Smith, and Burr, 1989). There are no ethnographic accounts of STS redesign that have captured the process as it actually occurs and documented how changes in managers' and employees' beliefs and behaviors are produced. This book is intended to fill this gap.

Data Collection

The primary method of data collection I used was participant observation, but it was supplemented by in-depth interviews, surveys, and focus groups. I spent on average two to three consecutive days per week at each site. At the Roseville site, I spent more than five hundred hours as a participant-observer over a seven-month period between March and October 1991. A year later, I conducted follow-up interviews with managers and employees to track the changes that had occurred. At the Santa Clara site, I spent more than seven hundred hours as a participant-observer from March 1993 to March 1994. I conducted follow-up interviews with managers and employees periodically over the next two years to track the changes I had documented in 1993–94.

My two main goals were to understand and become part of everyday life at each site and to document the process of work redesign as it unfolded. My emphasis during the first few weeks at each site was to develop relationships with managers and employees and to learn about the type of work (e.g., design or manufacturing) that was being redesigned. I took on actual jobs when possible. At the Roseville Surface Mount Center, I worked on the production line as a production operator and as an inspector. Like other employees, I first had to take a course on electrostatic discharge and pass a test to demonstrate that I knew how to prevent computer chips from being damaged. At first I worked alongside operators who taught me how to run the machinery and inspect boards for defects.

Eventually, I was able to assume an entire job on my own. I also accompanied production operators and supervisors to meetings about production and quality control and attended information meetings convened by management in the cafeteria (known as "coffee talks"). On several occasions I attended birthday and farewell parties for employees, both on- and off-site. Over seven months, I was able to observe, work, and talk with approximately half of the center's two hundred employees as well as all of its managers.

I always carried a pen and notepad to document observations and discussions with employees. Everyone knew who I was and what I was doing, and I assured them of confidentiality and anonymity when they wished. Working entire shifts at each site, week after week, enabled me to develop trusting relationships with employees and to continue conversations during breaks, lunchtime, and downtime about their lives, work, and the redesign.

At the Santa Clara Division, most of the work was abstract research and development done by engineers who spent most of their time at their computers writing software or in their laboratories inventing new hardware designs. It soon became clear that working a job as I did at Roseville would be nearly impossible. Instead I decided to spend time "shadowing" engineers as they went about their daily activities. I observed them at work on their computers and accompanied them to meetings—morning team meetings, quality control meetings, and meetings with other engineers to discuss new technical developments and current projects. I had ample opportunities to ask them questions about their work and what they thought about the division and the redesign. My notes show that I closely observed and interacted with most of the fifty-odd engineers in the R&D department and at least fifteen managers and supervisors.

At each site, I was given a cubicle with a desk and telephone where I could sit and write notes or plan my fieldwork activities. The cubicles were situated near the areas of the organizations I was studying. For instance, at Roseville, my cubicle was directly adjacent to the Surface Mount Center. At Santa Clara, my desk was located in the R&D section in one of the engineers' aisles. Working so close to employees provided valuable opportunities to collect data because employees would often stroll by and sit down to chat. These conversations often turned into lengthy and sometimes personal discussions. (Interestingly, as evidence of the fast pace of the restructuring at Santa Clara, my cubicle was moved four times over the course of the fieldwork. The common joke was that everyone's desk should have wheels.)

I also spent time with managers and supervisors as they went through their daily routines. A typical day included accompanying them on their rounds throughout the plant, as well as to weekly staff meetings and strategic business meetings and retreats. At each site, I was also able to participate in a variety of company rituals such as Friday afternoon barbecues held on the roof, seasonal holiday parties, "beer-busts" in the cafeteria to celebrate the conclusion of a successful project, and skits to affirm and strengthen HP's corporate culture.

I was always on the alert for critical incidents, unanticipated and stressful events that reveal behaviors and underlying beliefs that otherwise remained invisible. For example, at Roseville, one morning employees learned that millions of dollars worth of computer chips had been stolen from the site the previous night. The event set off a heated and anxious debate about whether the trusting HP environment had been fatally transgressed. For weeks, until the suspects were caught, employees were ordered to lock up valuable items. Employees took the assault personally and expressed an intense desire to return to the trusting environment they so valued.

I also collected many artifacts and documents such as organizational charts, internal communications and announcements, formal policy statements, newsletters, and other relevant historical information.

At each site, over the course of fieldwork I took detailed handwritten notes which I recorded in employees' own words. During some interviews I used a laptop computer to record conversations. Once I converted all fieldnotes to typewritten form, I entered them into a database which grew to nearly one thousand single-spaced, typewritten pages. I then indexed and analyzed the data by creating an indexing scheme and using it to categorize chunks of text. The indexing scheme was based on the study's research questions, as well as on other relevant issues and themes that emerged throughout the data-collection process.

After getting a grasp of how the organization worked, my focus shifted to the work redesign itself. I attended and documented kickoff meetings at which managers gave inspirational speeches about the need for the redesign and design teams' weekly meetings when they analyzed their organization's business, technical, and social systems. Whenever possible, I helped out by taking notes for the redesign facilitator or by copying and distributing memos to the group. At both sites I participated by conducting social analyses, which meant doing surveys, conducting focus groups, writing up the findings, and feeding them back orally. On several occasions I accompanied design team members on visits to customers. I attended off-site retreats at which the team members developed their proposals, special coffee talks where the design team presented proposals to the steering committees and to the rest of the workforce, and the design team's lunch and dinner celebrations held at local restaurants to celebrate their accomplishments.

In addition to being a participant-observer, I conducted interviews with managers and employees to get specific information and to chronicle changes in employees' viewpoints. Soon after I arrived at each of the sites, I conducted interviews with key managers and with leaders of the redesign effort. My primary objective was to become acquainted with the managers, explain the purposes of the research, secure their approval and guidance, and decide where to begin the research. I also used interviews to reconstruct the site's history, business situation, and plans for the redesign.

Over the course of the research, I conducted interviews with some managers and employees and with all members on the design teams. My goals were to understand how each individual viewed changes in the organization. These interviews were open-ended to allow employees to respond in their own words and to introduce new topics. I usually conducted interviews in person at the site, during breaks or lunch or at prearranged times. They typically lasted between fifteen and sixty minutes. Once relationships were established, I was also able to conduct interviews over the telephone.

At each site, I made it a priority to interview the design team members briefly at regular intervals to understand the subtle changes in their beliefs as they went through the redesign process. I asked why members had agreed to serve on the design team, what they thought about the value of the redesign, what obstacles to the redesign's success they perceived, and how the redesign was changing their perceptions of their own work roles. These interviews were open-ended and often led to conversations about topics such as the history of the site and the changing relationships among various departments and individuals.

Near or after the end of fieldwork at each site I conducted structured follow-up interviews with managers and employees to determine the impact of the redesign on each organization's structure, technology, policies and practices, and culture and to understand individuals' perceptions of the obstacles that remained. I selected individuals who represented the range of opinions that employees and managers held toward the redesign to minimize the chances of producing a biased conclusion.

I collected more data by conducting surveys and focus groups as part of each design team's social analysis. The questionnaire and focus groups were designed, conducted, and analyzed by the UCLA research team. We constructed questionnaires from findings from our ethnographic research to capture issues of trust between employees, interdependence, employees' investment in their work, and fair treatment.

I also held focus groups with employees to explore in depth the issues that emerged from the surveys. At Roseville, four focus groups explored issues about lack of trust, perceptions of inequity, and low morale among some employees. At Santa Clara, four focus groups were targeted to explore the new division's values: accountability, initiative, teamwork, and continuous learning.

A key benefit of conducting these surveys and focus groups was that it provided a way to expand my role from observer to active participant. After I collected and analyzed data from each site, I presented it to the design teams. This helped them understand the culture and which beliefs and behaviors would have to change, and it helped me by yielding vast amounts of new data about employees' beliefs and attitudes and confirming my findings, often adding substantial new detail and insights.

Let us now turn to the two case studies.

6 • The Roseville Surface Mount Center Redesign

In 1991, Roseville's Surface Mount Center occupied the south end of Building R5, one of five modern buildings that constitute HP's sprawling manufacturing facility in the rolling countryside just north of Sacramento. Part of HP's California Personal Computer Division, the Roseville Surface Mount Center was one of several within the company that produced printed circuit boards for HP's line of personal computers. Known as "motherboards," these boards house the semiconductor chips and a variety of other components such as capacitors and resistors that together function as the computer's brain. The mission of the center was to produce several varieties of high-quality boards at low cost and to achieve its competitive advantage by producing them in high volume.

The Surface Mount Center's name derived from its technology, which was relatively new. The older technology, known as "through hole," required operators to drill holes in a board and fasten components to its top side by threading a piece of wire through the holes and soldering its end to the board's bottom side. The technology worked, but it was inefficient because it rendered the bottom side of the boards useless. Using the new "surface mount" technology, operators soldered components directly onto the board's surface, freeing both sides for use.

The process of assembling a board started out at one end of the Surface Mount Center, where boards were neatly stacked in piles so they could be loaded into the first of a series of Fuji machines. Nicknamed "pick-'n-place" machines, these devices pick up components and then place them onto tiny droplets of solder with speed and precision impossible for human fingers to duplicate. As the boards continued down the production line, they were washed, dried, and hand loaded with connector shields and crystals too delicate to be handled by machine. The boards were then visually inspected, subjected to intense heat to measure their durability, and tested to see if they worked. Finally, the boards were shipped to the stockroom, from which they were ordered on demand and either used internally for the 286, 386, or 486 personal computers and networks assembled in Roseville or flown to HP's manufacturing facility in France, where they were assembled into PCs for the European market.

In early 1991, the Surface Mount Center was a newcomer to the Roseville site. A year earlier, the center, along with approximately half of its 140 permanent employees, had relocated from Sunnyvale, a city in California's high-tech Silicon Valley, to Roseville as part of HP's strategy to consolidate manufacturing of personal computers and networks. While in Sunnyvale, the center had grown quickly because of high demand for boards—so quickly, in fact, that its employees never had time to document the line's layout or the production process. As a result, knowledge of how the center actually ran was stored primarily in the memories of its employees. According to Kathy Hendrickson, an HP internal consultant, this accelerated pace was not surprising because rapid change had become the norm in HP's Personal Computer Group. She explained, "The attitude is that everything has to happen fast. Not only are you growing and changing ever faster, but you think you can't keep up because the marketplace is changing so fast. We never slowed down long enough to carefully understand it, plan it, document it, do it 'by the book' if you will!"

When they tried to reconstruct the center in Roseville, managers suddenly realized that they had no plan to follow. Hendrickson recalled, "After we tore it down in Sunnyvale and tried to put it back together in Roseville, we didn't know where any of the pieces went because we had never written it down. So when half of our Sunnyvale employees decided not to move to Roseville, we lost half of the recipe!" Only by relying on the memory of employees who transferred to Roseville were managers able to reconstruct the center in its new home. Once again, however, rising demand for motherboards took every moment of employees' time, leaving the production process undocumented for a second time.

Despite its rapid growth, the center was not competitive. Its production costs, measured in "cents-per-placement" (the cost of placing one component on a board), ran much higher than at other surface mount centers within HP. Its costs were greater still when compared with companies such as Texas Instruments that manufactured motherboards overseas, where labor costs were a fraction of Roseville's. Largely because of inefficiencies in its production process, the center simply could not manufacture boards fast enough to keep up with demand. As a result, customers' delivery requirements were not being met. Yet unless the center could produce boards in high volume, it could not achieve the economies of scale needed to make it competitive. It soon became clear to Roseville's management that something had to be done.

ORIGIN OF THE REDESIGN

In December 1989, Kathy Hendrickson came to work for Terry Pierce, the manufacturing manager of the California Personal Computer Division (CPCD) and the highest-level manager at Roseville's Surface Mount Center, to help improve the competitiveness of the CPCD's manufacturing facility. In that same year, along with Dennis Early, the center's production manager, she attended a workshop called "Work Redesign for the 90s" given by HP's internal consulting group called the Factory of the Future, where the two learned about STS redesign as a means to improve performance through self-managing teams of employees.[1] Hendrickson was especially drawn to STS redesign because it included employees in redesigning their own organization and was compatible with HP's egalitarian culture. She explained: "We need far greater levels of skills and commitment in our workforce than we've ever needed before to remain competitive in this environment. We figured the best possible way to achieve that would be to have employees design a new work system themselves, rather than have it be laid on them by someone else." Production manager Dennis Early was especially impressed by case studies of other companies presented during the workshop, which showed that STS redesign could lead to radical improvements in business performance.

Hendrickson and Early returned from the workshop convinced that work redesign could dramatically improve the center's competitiveness. Hendrickson discussed her ideas with Steve Tracy, the center's section manager, who enthusiastically agreed with her and promised to provide active support for the redesign. Next Hendrickson went to Terry Pierce, who was also convinced and gave Hendrickson permission to begin. But then, the two could not agree on where to start. Pierce maintained that because the materials used to create the boards represented the largest percent of the total production costs, the redesign should begin in the materials department. Hendrickson knew that the cost of producing the boards was also significant and that it could be reduced. More important, she explained, she had learned from a recent benchmarking trip to Digital Equipment Corporation that work redesign should begin at the core of the manufacturing process where the products were, as she put it, "touched by human hands and shipped out the door." Redesigning the core work, she thought, would exert a "pull" on the other departments within the division that supported the center, such as materials and engineering support,

---

1. The Factory of the Future advocated that HP employees attend the workshop in pairs (one internal consultant and one line manager) to ensure that redesign efforts gained the support of the managers in charge of the production process.

and create the need for them to follow suit. Pierce finally agreed with Hendrickson's analysis and gave her permission to proceed.

Hendrickson then discussed her ideas with some of the center's employees to determine their interest in redesigning their organization and working in teams. The employees she consulted were excited by the idea of broadening their skills and assuming more authority over decisions regarding their work. Hendrickson explained, "When we talked about self-managing teams in the very beginning, every one of them loved the concept of working in that kind of an environment. But they had been at a loss as to how to bring it about. They saw [the process of] redesign as a way to create it."

Hendrickson knew, however, that the redesign would have to be tied to business results to establish accountability with higher management. As stated in the center's 1991 "Hoshin Planning Table," a document used throughout HP to identify and track yearly objectives, the center's financial goal was to reduce its production costs by 15 percent to meet the CPCD's profitability objectives.[2] It would also have to decrease its production cycle to less than one day. These were formidable targets, which Hendrickson believed could be achieved only by enlisting employees' commitment and participation in redesigning and running the center. She and Early wrote out the formal business strategy for the center, which read: "Redesign the Surface Mount Center production to develop a structural, cultural and skill foundation for our organization that continually improves our performance in satisfying customers and ensures efficient work processes while improving the quality of our work life."

BEGINNING THE REDESIGN

In December 1990, Hendrickson formed a steering committee, consisting of eleven managers and engineers, to provide leadership and direction to the design team. The steering committee would also serve as a sounding board for the design team's ideas, approve or deny the team's proposed changes, ensure that the new design would enable the center to meet its business objective, and support the implementation of the new design.

Before handing over the redesign task to employees, the steering committee created a vision of how the "ideal" center would look after the redesign. Their images created an ambitious goal for the redesign. The managers and engineers envisioned that every employee would understand

2. "Hoshin" is a Japanese term derived from "Hoshin Kanri," which means "pushing down administration or management." A typical Hoshin planning table includes a concise description of an organization's business situation, its objective, target, goal, and strategies that will be employed to achieve the goal.

and support the center's purpose and direction and that all would work as a team to achieve its objectives. Every employee would be fully aware of the center's competition and be able to describe how the center was performing as well as his or her contribution to its competitiveness. The center would be equipped with leading-edge manufacturing technology. The cycle time for finished boards would be less than one day, and the number of defects would be greatly reduced. With fewer defects to correct, fewer employees would work in test and repair. Employees' behavior would demonstrate that HP cared for the environment and the community. Finally, the center's employees would be "winning and having fun."

In December 1990, Hendrickson formed the design team, representing a cross section of the organization, that would actually redesign the center. Design team members were elected by their peers through anonymous voting. Employees were instructed to nominate individuals not based on their popularity but on their being open-minded, respected by their peers, and opinion leaders. Nominees also had to have good communication skills and to be knowledgeable about the center's production process. The outcome was a diverse, eighteen-member team that included one manager, three engineers, three supervisors, and nine production operators from both day and night shifts. The team also contained diverse personalities. Hendrickson recalled, "We couldn't have ended up with a stranger mix! They ranged from being totally 'out there' to super-conservative. You name it, we had it. But the diversity contributed to [the team's] strength."

THREAT OF CONSOLIDATION

In early 1991, just after the design team was formed, managers learned that the Roseville Surface Mount Center might be consolidated with its sister center in Grenoble, France, as part of the company's emerging personal computer strategy. The decision had already been made to transfer one of the center's production lines to Grenoble to help meet a rising European demand for the high-end 386 machines. Production of some lower-end 286 boards had also been recently outsourced. This meant that there was only a single board, the one for the 486 product line, left for the center to build. Manufacturing only the boards for the 486 computers, however, would not provide the volume needed for the center to meet its lower cost targets. No longer able to provide a cost advantage, the company would have no logical alternative but to close the center and ship it to France.

The uncertainty about the center's future created a dilemma for the managers leading the redesign because it threatened to undermine the entire effort. Hendrickson recalled thinking, "Do we get the design team and later the whole organization riled up and rally them around taking a whole new approach to work, when the reality is that we might just have the rug pulled out from under us?" Deep down, the managers hoped that the redesign's results would persuade top management to consolidate manufacturing in Roseville, rather than in Grenoble. They also predicted that it would take months for the decision to be finalized. With the window open, if only for a limited time, Hendrickson and her managers decided to "push hopefully ahead."

ANALYZING THE CENTER AS A SYSTEM

In late 1990, the design team assembled for the first time to begin the redesign. Hendrickson arranged for the team members to participate in a simulation called the "Flying Starship Factory" that illustrated the advantages of a "high-performance" manufacturing environment that was designed by workers themselves over a traditional organization designed only by managers and engineers.[3] To demonstrate a traditional organization, employees sat around a mock assembly line that made papier-mâché "starships." Employees were told to follow strict instructions in carrying out their tasks—cutting, folding, and inspecting—and they were not allowed to communicate with each other or to rearrange their positions. At the end of the production run, only a few starships were of high enough quality to be delivered to the makeshift "customer," while most were riddled with defects and needed to be repaired. In the next run, however, employees were encouraged to communicate with each other and were allowed to redesign the production line to streamline their work. A "final assembler," for instance, told a "folder" who sat upstream that using a hard object such as a stapler to fold the starship, rather than folding it with his fingers, would produce a sharper crease and result in a better finished product. In another instance, a "painter" and a "cutter" decided to switch positions so that the painter could color the pieces of paper while they were still in one piece rather than after they had been cut into many little ones, thus saving time. After numerous suggestions were implemented and the second production run was completed, the value of employees' input was obvious. Only a fraction of the starships produced in this way were defective, and most of them had been successfully delivered to the "customer." The design team members cheered their accomplishments and immediately began to see the implications that this simulated redesign held for the center.

3. This simulation was adapted from an exercise devised by William O. Lytle and Associates and incorporates major themes from Marvin R. Weisbord's book *Productive Workplaces: Organizing and Managing for Dignity, Meaning, and Community* (San Francisco: Jossey-Bass, 1987).

Following the kickoff meeting, the design team members turned to conducting the business, technical, and social analyses.

The Business Analysis

The design team began by analyzing their business environment to achieve three main objectives: identify their customers' needs, find out how the center compared with its competition, and determine their stakeholders' level of satisfaction. To find out their customers' needs, they interviewed them. Many of their customers were just across the aisle in PC Assembly, where the center's circuit boards were installed into HP's line of personal computers. The members asked:

1. What product or service do you expect from us?
2. Are we meeting your expectations?
3. How do you gauge our performance?
4. What five things do we do right?
5. What five things do we do wrong?
6. What would you like to see changed?
7. Do you have any additional comments?

Much to their surprise, the design team discovered that their customers were unhappy with the quality of the boards they produced, which usually failed to meet expectations. These customers also reported that the center was not responsive enough to their needs—for example, when PC Assembly needed an extra set of a certain model of boards, it was told it would have to wait several days, if not weeks. This dissatisfaction made sense to the design team members, however, after they discovered that PC Assembly had set no clear standards for quality, cost, and responsiveness. In fact, despite their proximity, the team found that there was no formal communication between the center and its customers, either through regular visits or product reviews.

Team members also wanted to know how their center compared to other competitors in quality and on-time delivery. To find out, they conducted benchmarking trips to competitors such as Digital Equipment and NEC, plus visits to HP surface mount centers, where they made some critical discoveries that they called "key learnings" or "ah-ha's." One such key learning was that the Roseville Center's technology was already state-of-the-art, which meant it would not have to buy new technology to be competitive. They also found that the best surface mount centers had one continuous production line that ran on a "just-in-time" system with minimal inventory on hand at any given time. The lines were continuous, but they could be stopped by production operators to prevent defects from traveling down the line, and they had built-in buffers that allowed operators to vary their pace of work. Roseville's best competitors also used statistical process control techniques at key points in the production system that provided simple but real-time process feedback to operators so they could catch defects at their origins and standardize the production process. Although the design team members were impressed with what they saw and knew they could incorporate much of this knowledge in a newly designed production system, they also knew that for Roseville to survive, it would have to quadruple its volume and run at 85 percent of capacity—far greater than the current 56 percent.

As their final step in the business analysis, the design team members interviewed "stakeholders" (individuals other than customers who had vested interests in the center and who contributed in some way to its success) to determine their satisfaction with the center's performance. By interviewing thirteen such stakeholders from other departments, including procurement, process generation, engineering, and finance, design team members discovered that communication between departments was poor, thus limiting the degree to which they learned from each other. As a result, opportunities to share innovative process technologies or other sources of competitive advantage were being overlooked.

The Technical Analysis

Next, a detailed technical analysis was launched to identify and then eliminate the sources of variation that produced inefficiencies in the center's production system. To identify the sources of variation that came from outside the center, the design team first had to understand precisely how the parts that went into the boards, such as solder paste and semiconductor chips, flowed into the center from other departments such as materials and stores. They created a graphic representation called the "SMC Production Relationship Map" that looked like a complex maze but graphically revealed the center's relationship to each and every department within the CPCD, as well as to other HP divisions that affected its existence (see Figure 3).

To identify the internal sources of variation, the design team engaged all of the center's employees in the technical analysis by forming Process Improvement Teams ('PITs'), which included employees from each section of the production line. Each PIT documented the flow of boards through its section of the line and identified every variance (any unintended variation in the production process that affects quality, cost, responsiveness, or

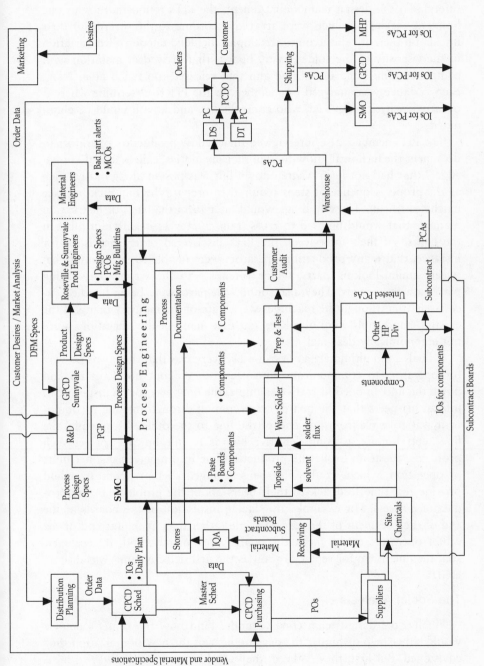

Figure 3. Roseville Surface Mount Center production relationship map

safety). To the design team's amazement, the PITs found more than one hundred variances, which were arrayed according to the severity of their impact on the critical outcomes. Examples included uncontrolled variation in the viscosity of the solder paste, boards that arrived at a station with components missing, and a glue gun that released too much glue. Next, each variance was analyzed by members of the PIT to determine where it occurred, why it happened, who controlled it, and how it could be eliminated.

The PIT members also interviewed their fellow production operators to document the technical know-how in their memories, called "tribal knowledge," that had not been written down but was passed along orally, such as the proper sequence of steps required to prepare the Fuji pick-'n-place machines to run. These findings would later form the basis of instruction manuals that would be used to cross-train employees in different jobs. In the course of their interviews, the PITs discovered other surprises—for instance, that many production operators were unable to differentiate between similar-looking parts, which often led to the wrong parts being placed on the boards. They also found that parts were being handled excessively, that though the machines were state-of-the-industry many of the existing hand tools were obsolete, and that many of the operations were not ergonomically designed.

A final—and ultimately a critical—discovery was that there was no way for operators to communicate with each other about problems up and down the line. In one illustrative example, the only way for an inspector to inform his peers that the boards were coming through missing a component was to walk from one end of the line to the other. Meanwhile, the line kept running, causing defective boards to pile up. To correct such problems, the team broke the production line into nineteen distinct units of operation, which would later be rearranged so that operators could provide real-time feedback to their peers about the problems in the production process. For example, by placing inspection of the boards at the end of each segment of the assembly line rather than at the far end of the center operators could check the boards immediately, and, if necessary, shut the line down for repair as soon as the first defective unit was discovered.

The Social Analysis

Finally, the design team tried to understand how the center's culture would either help or hinder the development of the new organization they envisioned. But first, they realized, they would have to find a way to measure the center's culture. Hendrickson called HP's Factory of the Future and some other HP divisions that had done work redesign for advice. She located two surveys that had been successfully used to conduct social analyses. An instrument called the "Job Diagnostic Survey" aimed to determine the fit between employees and their jobs (Hackman and Oldham, 1980). Another, called GAIL (Goal Attainment, Adaptation, Integration, and Long Term Development), attempted to measure the degree to which organizations carried out these four functions. Hendrickson considered using HP's annual on-line employee survey but decided against it because she felt that many of its questions had a paternalistic tone. Eventually, Hendrickson asked our UCLA research team to design a survey instrument for the social analysis. The timing was fortuitous because we were already on site studying the center's redesign effort. Working with Hendrickson and the design team, we formulated a questionnaire to identify and measure the assumptions, beliefs, and behaviors that were considered critical for the development of a high-performance organization, including the need for employees to feel they were treated fairly, to understand the competitive environment, and to trust each other as well as managers. The questionnaire was administered to the entire manufacturing floor, which in addition to the center included two other groups of employees: PC Assembly, where the personal computers were assembled, and Terminals, an older, established line that produced terminals for personal computers.

The survey findings revealed a stark and gloomy picture. The center scored lower than PC Assembly and Terminals on virtually every dimension that was explored, from confidence in the center's future to trust in their peers. The center's employees were far more worried about the CPCD's future than were employees in the other two areas. They were very concerned about the quality of their boards and believed that the production system prevented them from doing their jobs effectively. More worrisome, however, the center's employees distrusted managers, whom they believed withheld information from them about the center's future. They were also more anxious than employees in other areas about being laid off, despite HP's practice of employment security. The center's employees believed that their hard work went unrecognized and felt that they were treated less fairly than employees in other areas.

Hendrickson and Tracy scheduled a special day-long off-site meeting to review the survey findings with the design team members. As each finding was presented, the design team confirmed its validity. The findings were of great surprise and concern to Tracy, the center's section manager, who had assumed that employees' morale would be higher because the center had already succeeded in reducing its production costs. More seriously, the survey results suggested that the core values of the HP Way, which were critical to the success of the redesign (e.g., trust and fairness), had eroded beyond repair. Dismayed, Tracy exclaimed: "Are we going back to the laws of the jungle? Is this just survival of the fittest? We can't have team-work in this kind of environment!"

The design team spent several hours discussing the reasons behind the alarming findings. Employees explained that they had become concerned about poor quality after the technical analysis revealed over a hundred variances in the production system, each of which lowered quality and raised cost. "Once we knew what to look for," one member said, "variances just started popping out all over the place. It made us realize how far we had to go to be competitive." Their concerns were exacerbated by the realization that almost half (40 percent) of the center's employees—a higher percentage than in other factory departments—worked in non-value-adding test and repair. Employees also explained that they distrusted management because they received no information about the center's future. Ironically, as Tracy explained, he had shielded employees from information about the center's uncertain future to avoid causing alarm. The absence of information, however, had strengthened rumors that the center would be shut down, leading employees to worry about their own futures. One production operator explained, "We need more communication but instead we get less. Management needs to do a better job of communicating the turmoil to the floor. We need to be able to plan for the future." Rumors that the center could be shut down had already made many worry about being "excessed" and had reduced support for the redesign. One member said, "Everyone wants to do a good job, but their jobs are threatened. Everyone's afraid of downsizing—who will stay and who will go." The situation had been further exacerbated by Tracy's well-intentioned effort to spend less time on the floor to allow the teams to become more self-managing, which instead made employees feel that their hard work went unnoticed and unappreciated. One design team member grumbled, "In the division next door, when they reach their goals, they get pizza. We get nothing, not even a thank you." Surprised but enlightened, Tracy resolved to be more open with employees about the center's future and to share whatever news he had, even if the news was bad.

DESIGN WEEK

In April 1991, the design team assembled in the conference room of a nearby hotel for a week-long meeting they called "Design Week" to draw together the findings from the business, technical, and social analyses and to create a new organizational design for the center. Hendrickson set up the room to accommodate the eighteen design team members. Each member had a designated seat around a large U-shaped table and was given several books on teamwork and empowerment, a large blue binder filled with articles on work redesign and homework assignments, and a set of colored pens.

Throughout the week the team had to follow a set of ground rules for working together, which were displayed on a chart taped to the wall. All members were expected to participate fully, but only one person could talk at a time. Members were expected to take risks and to be sensitive to others. Decisions would be made by consensus, but members were expected to understand and unconditionally support all alternative views. Members were expected to share responsibility for facilitating the meetings and to help ensure their effectiveness. Any member who felt a meeting was going too slowly or was getting out of control was expected to call a "process check," similar to a "time-out," and halt the meeting. Finally, members were encouraged to give each other a "standing ovation," defined as an "ovation to be initiated by any member to acknowledge BRIL-LIANCE on the part of any teammate."

As a first step, the design team members generated a list of "hopes and concerns" for the redesign. Examples of hopes:

- We will save the Center.
- Morale will improve.
- We will achieve self-ownership.
- The benefit of our efforts will far exceed the cost.

Examples of fears:

- We will be rushed at the end.
- Business decisions regarding our future have already been made.
- We will be unable to grasp all we need to move ahead.
- We will be sabotaged by our peers.
- My ideas won't be considered because of my level.
- We are viewed as elitist.
- We intimidate others with our enthusiasm.
- Great ideas never get implemented.
- Some of us will not be around to see the results.
- Business conditions worsen and we drop.

To guide the design activities, Hendrickson used a model advocated by HP's Factory of the Future that looks like, and is appropriately called, the "Bull's-Eye" model (see Figure 4). (Figure 5 shows how Hendrickson adapted the model for the Roseville Surface Mount Center redesign.) At the center of the Bull's-Eye are two elements: the organization's purpose or mission, which is often represented by the customers' needs; and the orga-

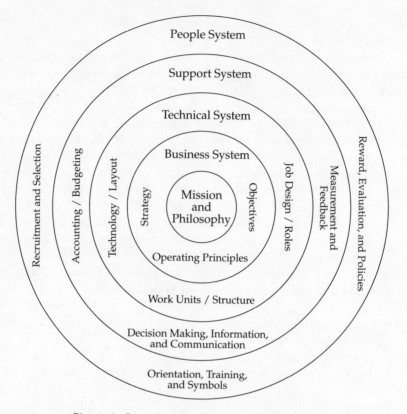

Figure 4. Organizational design: Bull's-Eye model

nization's vision or philosophy, which is often represented by its values. The outer rings of the Bull's-Eye represent the organization's major systems—business, technical, support, and people. Following the Bull's-Eye model, employees first identify an organization's purpose (or customers' needs) and vision (or values). They then develop the business strategies and objectives that make up a business system. As part of a technical system, employees then analyze elements such as the organization's technology, structure, and work roles. Next they examine systems of measurement and feedback, decision making, and communication that compose a support system. Finally, they analyze the people system, which includes an organization's culture and human resources policies and practices (e.g., reward, evaluation, and training strategies).

The first few days of Design Week were spent on the business system. After reviewing the findings from the business analysis, Hendrickson led the team through developing the center's new purpose, vision statement, and business strategies. (The organization's values were already provided

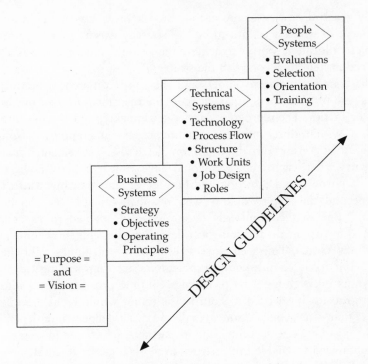

Figure 5. Roseville's Bull's-Eye model

by the HP Way.) As the team members brainstormed for possible purpose statements, Hendrickson wrote down their ideas on large pieces of poster paper which she taped to the walls. The team then spent hours debating and editing their suggestions until they agreed on the center's new purpose statement: "To satisfy our customers by manufacturing printed circuit assemblies that meet or exceed their technology, quality, responsiveness, delivery, and cost (otherwise known as 'TQRDC') expectations."

The team began developing the vision statement in the same way by brainstorming. They soon realized, however, that the same ideas were emerging—for example, one suggestion for a vision statement was "having satisfied customers." The discussion abruptly came to a halt as members realized to their dismay that they did not know the difference between a purpose statement, a vision statement, a strategy, and a tactic. Their confusion led to a prolonged discussion, and the team debated the semantic definitions of these words for several hours. Intent on resolving the issue, they closed the shades of the room to force themselves to concentrate. After drawing analogies to how the words "strategy" and "tactic" were used in military combat and looking up the words in the dictionary, they finally reached consensus. A vision, they agreed, was a "philosophical statement of where we want to be." A strategy was a "long-term plan of action to allocate resources to achieve the vision," and a tactic was a "specific action item to accomplish the strategy."

The team's struggle to understand the subtle differences between the terms paid off. Members began categorizing their ideas into visions, strategies, or tactics. Their progress accelerated quickly, and the exercise was finished within thirty minutes, eliciting cheers and applause from the group. A supervisor read aloud the completed vision statement, which had five parts. First, each employee would have a clear understanding of the center's purpose and direction and how he or she contributed to its success. Second, the center would be what members called a "learning organization," one that continuously monitored and adapted to its changing business environment, technological developments, and surrounding environmental trends. Third, employees resolved to "do things right the first time" and focus on preventing problems rather than solving them (also known as "firefighting") by providing real-time process control information to those who needed it. Fourth, the center would be aware of—and better than—its competition. Finally, a well-defined interdependency would exist between the center and its partners, which would be measured and optimized to enable both parties to work together to meet their customers' TQRDC expectations.

Next the team identified four strategies to develop an organization that could eliminate or control variances at their source. First, they recommended that the center accomplish its TQRDC objectives by establishing work groups. Second, they suggested the establishment of cross-functional communication groups with representation from all key partners to focus on specific issues such as training or new product development. Third, they suggested making employee development an ongoing process. Finally, they would develop and implement an ongoing redesign plan.

Learning Statistical Process Control

After completing the purpose, vision, and strategy statements, the team turned to redesigning the center's technical system. Several engineers on the team began discussing how to apply Statistical Process Control (SPC) to the production line, while silence fell over the rest of the group. Finally, one team member raised his hand and asked sincerely, "What exactly is SPC?" Team members rose and gave him a standing ovation for his honesty and courage in speaking for the group. In response, several engineers began reviewing the technical principle that variances should be controlled at their source. It soon became clear, however, that even the engineers on the team did not agree on the definitions of terms such as "variance" and "source." A somber mood fell over the group. "How are we going to implement SPC if we don't even understand it?" asked one team member. Others chimed in agreement. Speaking for the group, Tracy acknowledged, "We're befuddled. I'm at a loss too. The educational level needed to understand this stuff is too high . . . other companies have statisticians advising them on how to do this, and we're trying to do it ourselves! We may have to take a step back."

The team decided to break for lunch and discuss the standstill. Members concluded that they did not understand the concepts because they were too abstract. Hendrickson suggested that the team postpone the theoretical discussion of SPC for the time being and instead find real-life examples of variances by examining the flow of work through the production line, one unit of operation at a time. The team members followed her advice. After lunch, they broke up into groups and wrote down the variances they had found earlier during the technical analysis on yellow sticky notes. At one point, the team member who had questioned the meaning of SPC realized that what he had written (variation in the viscosity of the solder paste he used at his machine) was an example of a variance. "I've guess I've been doing SPC all the time. . . . I just didn't know what it was called!" he exclaimed. He received another standing ovation from the team.

After attaching the sticky notes containing the variances to a blueprint of the entire production line that stretched from wall to wall, members picked up colored pens and redrew the boundaries of the work units—not around technology (e.g., similar machines grouped together) but around flows of information. Redesigning the line around channels of communication would enable employees to inform each other quickly about defects traveling down the line and to track and control variances at their source. When finished, they stood back and cheered, clearly proud of their accomplishment.

Although it made sense from a technical standpoint, the process of redrawing the layout of the assembly line brought up some sensitive social issues pertaining to prestige and job status. One team member who worked in the front end of the center, where the most highly technical and difficult work was done, suddenly realized that his job had been redrawn to the back end of the line, where more mundane, tedious work was performed by people who he had once said jokingly worked like "robotic teddy bears." "I'm getting lonely already," he moaned aloud. His concerns were acknowledged and defused when his peers rose to their feet and gave him a standing ovation for admitting his reluctance to move to a lower-status area. They also presented him with the "Whining Award" to tease him good-naturedly for being pompous.

Defining a Team

After defining boundaries of the new work units, the next step was to determine the relationship between the units and the work teams. Behind schedule but determined to resolve the issue, the team ordered pizza and beer and worked well into the evening. Hendrickson began the discussion by voicing her assumption that teams would be based on the work units. Some members agreed. Others felt that a team should include an entire assembly line. The discussion soon became an emotional debate about the subjective meaning of the term "team." One member named Bob, who had until now been silent, explained that to him, the word "team" implied competition and thus created barriers. "Calling us a team is like calling your kid Biff . . . it becomes a self-fulfilling prophecy. Eventually all the teams would be competing with each other—is that what we want?" Several suggested the term "unit," which others rejected because, they explained, "it doesn't create a family feeling." Finally, the team settled on the term "group."

The next question was who to include in a work group. Should it include supervisors, engineers, technicians, and even those across the building in Storage? The team finally decided that a group should be as broad in scope as necessary to enable all of those who shared the common purpose of producing the product and controlling variances. This raised yet another concern: if supervisors and production operators were on the same team, how could supervisors evaluate the production operators? This issue was postponed for a later discussion.

In the end, the team decided that there would be three types of groups. Work groups would be responsible for producing the product and controlling variances. Problem-solving groups would be made up of the already existing PITs and focus exclusively on technology issues. Finally, cross-functional groups would include members from every work group plus key partners outside the center and would facilitate communication and management of cross-functional processes.

By midweek the team was behind schedule and conducted a process check. They concluded that they had bogged down too frequently in semantics and around emotional issues, as evidenced by the lengthy discussions about the words "strategy," "tactic," and "team." The team members decided that they needed to improve their ability to detect emotionally charged issues before they erupted into heated discussions and to reach consensus on issues more quickly. The next morning, to acknowledge the difficulty—but necessity—of resolving semantic and emotional issues, one supervisor brought in a brown grocery bag filled with what he called "tools" to weather the next confusing or heated discussion. One by one he pulled out a dictionary, a thesaurus, a fire extinguisher, a plastic bottle labeled "bullshit repellent," boxing gloves, Alka Seltzer tablets, and Kleenex tissues. "And if all else fails, you can put the bag over your head!" he joked.

Redefining Roles

The most difficult issues surfaced on the last day of Design Week, when the team redefined the roles of section manager, supervisor, engineer, technician, and production operator to support self-managing teams. The first role to be redefined was that of section manager. The exercise began on a humorous note that illustrated Tracy's commitment to pushing responsibility and authority down into the organization. As a joke, the team presented Tracy with a list, which they had prepared the previous evening, of his new responsibilities. He would now—among other menial activities—make the coffee, take out the trash, mop the floor, and park the cars. Tracy accepted the list in mock pain as the team erupted in laughter. Once the joke was over, the team, working with Tracy, redefined his role in all seriousness. At Tracy's request, he would now be called the business manager and would focus not on managing the center but on strategic planning and scanning the environment to identify business opportunities that would help the center grow. He would also keep employees abreast of changes in the division's strategic direction so they could better plan their futures.

Next the team redefined the role of supervisor, who would be called "coach." One supervisor presented a list he had created that illustrated how supervisors would do less planning, leading, answering, controlling, decision making, and delegating. They would concentrate on transferring their skills, training employees in how to obtain resources, asking questions, team-building, and relinquishing authority to empower the group. The team cheered the list and gave the supervisor a standing ovation. "I like the idea of working for a supervisor like that," one member said. Another pointed out, "Actually, I can see how when we become self-managing, we won't need a supervisor at all!"

Next to be redefined were the roles of engineers and maintenance technicians. Engineers would retain their current roles but in addition would become active members of the work group and participate more in its daily activities. Engineers would also begin training production operators in everything from production planning to SPC so that eventually operators could do such activities themselves. Maintenance technicians, in addition to their current roles, would also become active group members.

Moreover, they would become cross-trained in maintenance skills so they could fix a variety of machines rather than a select few and would transfer their knowledge of equipment control and failure prevention to the group.

The last role for the team to redefine was that of production operator, which included most of the team. Eager to expand their responsibilities, members shouted out suggestions while a supervisor jotted them down on the board. The list soon contained nineteen responsibilities, many of which had previously belonged to management. For example, production operators would now make daily tactical decisions, manage work in progress, select their own group members, evaluate their peers, seek out production support when necessary, participate in setting product specifications and parameters, control quality and variances, and continually increase their knowledge of the business.

After the list was completed, the team stared at it for several moments in silence, comprehending the vast increase in responsibilities. Finally, one member commented, "That's a lot. How on earth are we going to convey this to everyone?" The ensuing discussion revealed the team's concern that not all employees would be willing and able to accept the new responsibilities. "The bad apples won't buy into this. They won't do all that," one member said. "What about those who don't speak English well?" another asked, referring to the Filipino population. The controversy grew when several temporary, or "flex-force," employees on the team admitted that they too were unwilling to commit to the added responsibilities—not because they did not want to, but because they felt that HP was not increasing its commitment equally to them in return. (Flex-force employees can work only two years for the company. While they agree to this policy when they sign on, many flex-force employees want to work permanently for HP and don't want to leave when the time comes.) "You're asking for a lot of investment. I don't mind doing all that—that's why I'm on this team—but why should I when I'll be forced to leave in a few months?" asked a flex-force employee named Linda, who had already worked at Roseville for over a year. Tension escalated when one manager suggested that flex-force employees were less invested than permanent employees because they knew they would be staying for only a limited time. "That's not true," one exclaimed. "Permanent employees are like the family cat; they think, 'You can't get rid of me.' They're the ones who aren't invested!" By now the discussion had become hurtful and accusatory. "Process check! Everyone take a deep breath," Hendrickson shouted. Everyone did, and in the subsequent discussion the team recognized that temporary employment was yet another thorny issue that could not be overlooked but would not be resolved easily. The team decided to form a task force to investigate the issue further and moved on.

The final topic of Design Week was what the team called the "People System," which included rewards, evaluations, selection, orientation, and training. The team decided that rewards should be recognizably linked to performance, skills, and knowledge and be based on group in addition to individual performance. They also suggested some form of localized profit sharing in addition to the company-wide profit sharing to reward the center when it exceeded its goals. The team decided to explore ways to evaluate entire groups in addition to individuals and ways the customer could play a role in evaluating the group. They suggested that evaluations, in addition to their traditional purpose, should be means to offer constructive criticism. They recommended eliminating HP's relative ranking system, which was perceived as a "zero-sum game" that discouraged teamwork because it forced individuals' performance into a normal distribution and evaluated employees based on how they compared with each other. Instead, they suggested developing a ranking system based on absolute performance criteria they developed themselves that would enable everyone to obtain the same high ranking. This system would work in conjunction with newly developed PC software that would enable group members to give each other anonymous feedback.

On the topic of selection, the team recommended that until work groups became self-managing, they would still have supervisors. But these supervisors should be selected by a panel made up of the business manager, other supervisors, and group members. Work groups would select their own members using behavioral interviewing techniques, which members would learn through a workshop. If a group member's performance was found to be below standard, the group members would act as a support system and help the individual improve his or her performance. Should an individual's performance fail to improve, however, a group could recommend to its supervisor that the employee be found a different job.

The team decided that new employee orientation should be the responsibility of two cross-functional groups, the training group and the social group. New hires would receive a "holistic view" of the center that would include coverage of its business, technical, and social systems, which team members explained had been invaluable in helping them understand the "bigger picture." Finally, the team recommended that adequate training be provided to all employees to equip and prepare them to take on the additional tasks and responsibilities that would be required of each employee to achieve the center's new vision.

Over the course of the week, the team encountered policies and practices that they wanted to change—for example, they wanted to eliminate the relative ranking policy, expand job classifications, and reconsider the flex-force employment policy. Hendrickson explained that these policies were governed by Corporate HP and would be difficult, if not impossible, to change. Nevertheless, task forces were organized to investigate possible alternatives as well as Corporate's willingness to sanction policy changes that would be made on an experimental basis.

Design Week ended on Friday afternoon at a nearby Mexican restaurant, where the team gathered around a large table laden with margaritas to celebrate their efforts. Feeling exhausted but accomplished, team members tried to predict how their peers would respond to their proposal. Most important, they agreed, would be overcoming employees' skepticism that the redesign was not "just another program" and convey to them how this redesign was different from other efforts. This led to an extended conversation about ways the team members themselves thought the redesign was unique. "It includes us!" said one. "Instead of just engineers and managers on the team, the workforce is too." "That's made me feel much more like an equal," said another, who shared an experience: "A couple of days ago, I passed Terry [the manufacturing manager] in the hallway. He joked about my wearing shorts. I said, 'Yeah, and these are my work clothes!' I never would have done that before." One production operator commented, "That STS stuff . . . I can't believe we learned all that. At first I didn't understand all those fancy words and philosophies. Kathy kept saying, 'Wait, wait, you'll get it.' Near the end, I finally did!" Another commented, "This redesign is home-grown . . . it grew from the inside. . . . Not like a couple of months ago," he said, referring to a recent training program for managers, "when those consultants came in and tried to teach managers how to be 'empowering.' The effect lasted for two days, and then managers went back to managing like they always did. Meanwhile, the consultant walked away with his check and got on the plane!" Others pointed out that the redesign was more radical than any they had ever seen. "None of the other attempts to change things around here changed the way the whole Surface Mount Center looked," one said. "Things were done in small areas, but never a whole system change."

After several speeches, a few tears, and much laughter, Hendrickson presented gifts and awards that were symbolic of the design team members' contributions during the week. She also presented each member with a redesign tool kit to encourage members to share the redesign experience with their peers. Each tool kit included a dictionary, a thesaurus, a box of tissues, pens, and a pad of paper.

After the design team members had gone home, Hendrickson reflected on the growth she had seen in them. "At the beginning, there were some on the team who just weren't used to looking at the world this way. It was really tough. We'd be zooming along on this plane, really getting into something, when a couple of people would make a statement or ask a question that made it clear that they really weren't getting it. But as the team formed and came together, they developed beautifully in terms of slowing down and reaching back to take others' hands and help them along. Then, somewhere along the way, all of those differences went away!"

Hendrickson also reflected that involving employees in redesigning the organization had become more difficult than she and other managers had anticipated. "People who were usually so quiet just came alive!" she commented. "Like Bob—the guy who didn't like the word team . . . and Linda, the temp who got mad at HP's flex-force policy. They've all just become much more vocal and questioning of authority," she commented, referring to their suggested policy changes, which Hendrickson knew would be difficult to make. She said she thought there would be no turning back to the way things were: "It's like they all now have an awareness, or a consciousness about all the other changes that have to be made. They're constantly looking around and asking, 'Who else do I affect?' It's like letting the tiger out of the cage. There will be no going back now. We're too far. I'm afraid if we tried to go back to the way things were, there would be mass regression."

FINAL PROPOSAL

The design team returned to the site a week later to present its proposal to the steering committee. For most members, this was the first time they had spoken to a group of managers. "Managers are used to this kind of stuff, but we never speak in public, let alone to a group of *managers!*" one exclaimed. In the days preceding the presentation many confided that they were "nervous as hell." One team member explained how they tried to overcome their anxiety: "We've been reasoning with ourselves that if we really believe in the new design—which we do—we should have no trouble explaining it to others, regardless of whether they're our peers or high-level managers." The team members prepared a set of overhead transparencies summarizing their proposed changes and practiced presenting their sections to each other during lunchtime and breaks. When the morning finally arrived, several employees who were still nervous had to take deep breaths, and others stammered while they talked. Yet the presentation went smoothly. The steering committee suggested few changes and commended the team's work. According to Hendrickson, it was "less like a proposal and more like an update." The steering committee also gave them permission to present the proposal to the remainder of the workforce.

The design team presented the proposal to the workforce in early June 1991. A question-and-answer session following the hour-long presentation revealed employees' reactions to the proposal. Their major concern, exactly as the design team had anticipated, was that this redesign was no different from past programs or efforts to change management styles or improve performance. One woman said, "I like most of the stuff I'm hearing, but we've heard a lot of these buzzwords before—like teams, quality, and communication. Usually these efforts last about three to six months, but then you get new managers and they go away. How is this going to be any different from the past? "

The design team members responded to their peers' concern by sharing their observations on the last evening of Design Week. They explained that they believed this redesign was different because employees had created the new design themselves and that teams would eventually control the entire production process. Managers also tried to help convince employees that the redesign's effect would be long term by stressing that employees themselves would reap much of the benefit through the extensive training that would raise their skills. Tracy, the center's section manager, said, "Look . . . there are no assurances that managers here now will be here in six months, but that's not important because the redesign training is targeted to the individual. Our commitment is to teach you this process so that you will have a higher value while you're here, as well as when you walk out of here. You will keep that with you wherever you go, and it will help you succeed."

A temporary employee on the design team elaborated on Tracy's point: "The redesign training is not to solve specific problems in each shop but to raise us above entry level so you can go back to your office, shop, or machine to correct problems there. If you go to Intel or NEC tomorrow, you'll benefit from the training there. So it's really a development process. If you're here at HP for two days, HP will benefit for two days. If you're here at HP for two years, HP will benefit for two years. But you're getting the most out of the training that will be offered."

Pierce, the manufacturing manager, reiterated: "This ain't just another program. It's the way we want to do the work. You have management's buy-in from my level on down that this is the way we will do business."

SUMMER SCHOOL

In late June, while the production line was being reconfigured according to the new design, the center shut down and its 140 permanent employees met for a week-long meeting in an auditorium at the local fairgrounds to go through their own condensed version of Design Week. The purpose of the event, dubbed "Summer School" by the design team, was to teach employees the basics of work redesign and develop the new work groups.

On the first day the workforce split up into four groups and went through the Flying Starship Factory exercise. They came to the same conclusions as had the design team—that the center's performance could be dramatically improved by establishing better channels of communication up and down the line and by implementing employees' suggestions. At various points during the simulation, Hendrickson gave brief lectures on STS redesign theory to help employees make the connection between the simulation and the center. For instance, after the second run of the Starship simulation, Hendrickson stood up in front of the group and captured everyone's attention when she said: "Did anything seem familiar to how things work back in the Surface Mount Center? Doesn't that make you stop and think how *darn good* things could be if we got rid of problems like this? We could improve our cents-per-placement. The theory behind what you just did is STS. It's based on the idea that every organization has three dimensions—business, technical, and social. HP is a technology-driven company, so we typically try to solve every problem with a technical solution—for example, by bringing in new equipment. But what does that do to the business system? Doesn't it cost more? And what does it do to the social system? Will it replace five people? Work redesign is getting the system back in balance. And who do you think knows how to do that better than you? That's right, nobody! In a high-performance organization, you—the experts—help redesign the organization."

At other points throughout the week, the employees interviewed their customers from PC Assembly who had been invited to come to the fairgrounds to sit on the customer panel. Just as the design team had done, employees created purpose and vision statements for their new work groups as well as for themselves individually. They listed their hopes and fears, discussed them as a group, and went through exercises designed to help them go through change, break down barriers, and improve interpersonal relationships. They also signed what were called "interaction agreements" designed to ensure that individuals would confront each other directly when conflict arose rather than go to a supervisor. Finally, using the design team's proposal as an example, each new work group redesigned the flow of work in its area, developed new process measures, and mapped out the flow of information that would help reduce variances at their source.

Watching the new work groups redesign their work areas was very difficult for the design team members, who by virtue of the time and energy they had invested during Design Week had become very attached and partial to their particular design. One lamented: "It killed me to stand by and watch them struggle as we had—I wanted to intervene—hand them our design and tell them, 'This is the best way to do it.' It was really hard for me to accept that our way was not the best way and that they had to come up with their solutions for how their groups would run." They knew, however, that only by struggling through the process themselves would their peers reach the same levels of understanding and commitment to the new way of working.

Encountering Diversity

Summer School illustrated the difficulties of attempting to convey work redesign principles and recreate the design team's experience with a large, diverse workforce. The design team was highly motivated and members had been selected for qualities such as open-mindedness and communication skills, whereas the 140 employees in the large auditorium ranged in ethnicity, motivation, and willingness to change. In one instance, a supervisor asked an employee who had worked in the center for years to suggest a vision statement. She refused, shaking her head. The supervisor explained to her, "You can't always rely on the talkers for participation. We need everyone's input here." Embarrassed and offended, she responded: "Don't you dare call on me! I'm not a talker. I don't know why not, and even if I did, I couldn't explain it. It's nothing new, I've been that way ever since I was a little girl in school."

Over the course of the week, however, the activities and exercises designed to break down barriers and encourage teamwork began to work. Employees who had worked in the center for years but who had never exchanged a word found themselves sitting next to each other for the first time. One exercise raised the issue of racism, which several employees confirmed had never before been openly discussed. The issue surfaced when employees were asked to describe how they thought they would have to change to work in the new organization. After several commented that they would need to work more closely with their peers, one operator, referring to the Filipinos who worked in the center, said, "That's going to be hard when some people stay in their little cliques and refuse to get involved in group activities." Another pointed out that it was difficult to communicate with those who had limited fluency in English. "Yeah, and aren't willing to learn," another quipped. A design team member stood up and said, "That's not true. They are willing to learn. Lina [a Filipina] brings a dictionary to work and is always asking me what words mean, and I try to explain." At this point, a Filipina stood up and said: "Being a minority, I feel discriminated against. People don't say hello to you when you come in. I'm friendly. My English has improved because I married a Caucasian. But for others it's not easy to learn. We stay together when people treat you differently. It's hard to talk about because it seems like complaining, so we don't say too much. But we are good workers, just as good as anyone else. There is no reason we should be treated differently, just because we don't look and talk the same."

After she spoke, several Latinos stood up and shared similar feelings. Over the course of the discussion, reflecting on their experiences, several design team members described how they had learned the importance of bringing everyone along as a team. One said, "That's the only way we are going to survive. We'll only be as strong as the weakest link." By the end of the exercise, the group understood that the barriers that existed were not based on ill will and would have to come down. As a first step, employees agreed, language classes should be offered to overcome communication barriers. The Filipino and Latino employees expressed an interest in attending. Employees also agreed on the need to create classes on topics such as teamwork and interpersonal relations to help everyone become more sensitive and better able to work as a team.

This activity had a profound impact on Hendrickson as well. "I'm beginning to realize that this whole redesign is about breaking down stereotypes," she explained. "Stereotypes about personality types, job classifications, and roles . . . about all the barriers that exist and that are actually necessary parts of the system but then work against you when you start to break it down. This process, more than anything else in my life, has taught me to see that boxes around people are wrong! Or, that there's just really only one big box! I now have a much broader acceptance of and deep belief that everybody has something incredible to offer."

Summer School came to a close on Friday afternoon. The center's managers and employees returned to the factory for an ice cream social in the cafeteria.

IMPLEMENTING THE NEW DESIGN

In the weeks following Summer School the first steps were taken to implement the new organizational design. With the production line reconfigured, employees began working in their new groups. A transition team was appointed to guide the implementation of the new design, and a training coordinator was named. Seven new cross-functional groups, called counsels, were formed to address specific issues: business; electrostatic discharge; environment, health, and safety; social; training; new product and process introduction; and materials.

Over the next few months, the Surface Mount Center's employees participated in a wide variety of training sessions designed to prepare them to work in self-managing teams. Supervisors began taking "Zapp" workshops based on the book *Zapp! The Lightning of Empowerment* to help them make the transition to being coaches.[4] Task forces would be formed to investigate Corporate HP's willingness to sanction changes in the center's reward and evaluation systems. The cross-functional training counsel began developing and coordinating classes for employees in a wide variety of topics such as English, reading, writing, production planning, behavioral interviewing, interpersonal relations, and Statistical Process Control.

In the months that followed Summer School, a small but significant number of employees, many of whom had been on the design team, began exhibiting a wide range of new behaviors that could be described as "empowerment." The first noticeable difference was that employees were more motivated and enthusiastic than they had been before, which many attributed to their broadened perspectives. One production operator said, "Interviewing our stakeholders as part of the business analysis made me interested in the business aspects of our center—who our customers are and what they want. Before, all I cared about was how much work was coming down the line." Another explained, "My wife says that when I was in redesign I had this high, this constant high. I was off the line, interviewing people, and people were listening to my ideas! Then after redesign was over it was just kind of a letdown."

Gradually, employees began taking on more responsibility and initiative and making decisions on their own rather than looking to their supervisors. One production operator gave an example: "When the scheduler calls to tell us it's time to start running a new product, he'll ask us, 'Can you see if you have the materials?' We used to have to go to the supervisor and say, 'The scheduler called and wants to change the schedule. Is it OK if we go ahead and build that?' Now we make the decisions ourselves and say, 'Sure, we can do that.'" Employees also took on other tasks previously reserved for supervisors, such as gathering and analyzing production data, which they displayed on the wall at the center's entrance. One said, "Before the redesign, only certain people would do all the different types of data collecting and charting it and making reports for management. With the redesign all of us are learning how to do those things."

No longer dependent on supervisors, many production operators began to look to their own teams for advice. One explained: "The redesign made us aware that a team works better than an individual person. Our mentality has changed. Out on the floor we always felt we had to go ask the supervisor. Now we tell ourselves, 'Let's ask the team—see what everyone is thinking.'" She provided an example: "Often we're behind schedule and decide we need to work overtime. Now we figure out as a team how much

4. See William C. Byham's *Zapp! The Lightning of Empowerment* (New York: Harmony Books, 1988).

overtime we need, like two hours or a day or whatever. That used to be strictly dictated by supervisors."

Bypassing the supervisor gave employees more flexibility, which translated into increased efficiency. An engineer explained: "Before, production operators had little authority to make decisions about when to stop the line and ask an engineer for help. They'd have to call their supervisor over and wait for him to shut down the line and call an engineer. Now, they stop the process and go straight to the engineers when they need help. So now we've got unsupervised production operators working directly with process engineers on an as-needed basis. That was never done in the classic HP environment and was practically unthinkable before the redesign." This efficiency also worked in reverse. The engineer explained: "Before, engineers felt they had to deal with supervisors, and supervisors felt they needed to know everything that was going on. Now, when engineers want to do something, they go talk directly with the production person responsible for that particular process or machine and work it out with them. Rather than worry about bureaucracy or getting permission, they go right to the area and get it done."

Employees also began going beyond the boundaries of their work areas to identify the root causes of problems—another task traditionally reserved for supervisors. One supervisor who had been on the design team gave an example: "When boards fail their final inspection in Test, operators now travel up the line to find out why, rather than accept the condition of the board as is and toss it into the rework pile." He added, "They used to see things in little niches and operated within narrow borders. Now they see a whole system from top to bottom and analyze upstream changes that could improve their group's performance."

Production operators attributed their investigative behavior to a better understanding of their production system. "Mapping out the production line during the technical analysis made me understand what goes on at the front end," one said. Another explained, "The Flying Starship Factory exercise we did in Summer School made us much more aware of what goes on. Before, we were only focused on our own little areas. Now, we're focused on the whole process, how everything actually works hand in hand. If one little wheel down here doesn't work right it affects the whole process, where before . . . well, that's something we learned with that Starship. If you didn't fold your little fold properly, the guy down the line couldn't put it together! But before, our mentality wasn't that way. We used to think, 'Well, as long as I'm doing a good job in my area, that's all that counts.' But it isn't all that counts. Everyone has to do a good job all the way down the road. You've got to do your job well so the next person can carry it on and do his job well."

Employees also began to seek information from other departments. An engineer gave an example: "We're trying to improve the documentation in our mechanical assembly test area, which requires getting information from the engineers upstairs. Before, folks' hands were tied and they couldn't walk beyond their work area. They'd need a supervisor to run interference. Now nothing stops them . . . they are going beyond the boundaries of their work areas to find the information they need."

With a greater sense of confidence, many production operators began standing up for themselves and questioning authority. One operator who had been on the design team said, "Now, when a supervisor asks me to attend a meeting but I'm tied up in a production run, I tell him, 'I can't.' " Another said that when engineers arrive at the line and want to do experiments, he does not hesitate to tell them, "No you can't right now because we're four thousand boards behind, we don't have time, and we're short of people. Can you come back when we're caught up?"

Employees also began to exhibit greater flexibility as a result of cross-training and documenting the production process. A production operator explained: "It used to be that whichever area or department you worked in, that was your assignment. That's where you stayed and spent your eight hours. Through the cross-training we've learned all the different processes, which made us more flexible. Now everyone on the team can do everyone else's job. That means if someone's out sick or on vacation, you can take their place and there's no lull in production." Another operator said, "We used to have a few experts and a lot of Indians. Now we have lots of experts."

Summing up the changes he saw in employees, one manager said, "They really started caring about what they were doing and stepped up to the plate to take charge instead of just coming in to collect a paycheck. They began taking on more responsibility and initiative than ever before rather than just being handed responsibility and being told what to do."

As the center's employees became more empowered, they began to encounter resistance from employees in other areas of the division. This occurred most often when production operators ventured out to gather information from supervisors in other departments who were unfamiliar with the concept of self-managing teams. A production operator explained: "Several times now, I've gone to talk to a supervisor in another area about a problem. They'd say, 'What are you talking about? I need to talk to your supervisor.' Or, they'd go, 'Well, OK,' but instead of coming back to you with the information you need they'd go back to your supervisor and bypass you. They wouldn't even keep you in the loop any more. They would think that they had to deal with your supervisor. They didn't want to deal with us."

One production operator described the difficulty of being the only self-managed group in a large site: "Becoming self-managed worked out pretty well through our production area, but it got really difficult when we started dealing with other people not tied directly to you. They weren't accustomed to self-managing, or team-based or anything like that, they weren't even aware of anything about it. When you're the only group that's self-managed and team-based, it's practically impossible to deal with these other fifteen or sixteen groups out there that aren't. It's really tough. Nobody understands what's going on."

Echoing a similar observation from his point of view, Tracy said: "A lot of our problem right now is not so much the production area being able to be flexible and meet the challenge, as the rest of the division understanding what it means to them. We have product engineers from other departments who are having a hard time understanding what the redesign means to their processes and their needs. Marketing is still trying to understand what that means for responsiveness to delivery, etc."

Several members of the design team pointed out that diffusing the work redesign principles throughout the site would not be easy. One technician who was on the design team explained: "This type of relationship—feedback from operator-level workers to their supervisors and personal one-on-one between co-workers—is new. Not everyone's ready for it. This stuff means you have to be ready to break the rules, tear down the walls, and open up the roof to the blue sky."

Resistance also surfaced within the center from engineers and supervisors who had difficulty when operators exercised their newfound sense of authority. One production operator explained: "Sometimes engineers come out and want to do experiments on the line. Instead of asking us, they go directly to the supervisor. Instead of asking if we can fit them in, they say to us, 'We want to do this experiment.' When I say, 'No you can't right now because we're behind and we don't have time,' they go whine to our supervisors, 'Woowoowoowoo, they won't let us do our experiment.' And it's like, well wait a minute! You come to us, we give you an answer, you don't like our answer so you go crying to somebody else?!"

Some supervisors, especially those who had not been on the design team, resisted operators' display of authority. One supervisor simply explained that he "didn't support the philosophical principles underlying STS design." A production operator complained: "Some supervisors never did buy into the redesign, and I don't think they ever will. They weren't willing to play from day one. It's been really tough dealing with them. They'd come over and say, 'I want this, and this, and this done.' And I'd say, 'No.' They'd look at me as if to say, 'Who are you to tell me no? I want it done this way, and you do it now.' "

Although employees complained about the resistance they encountered, it did not stop them from exercising their own new roles. Soon the benefits of their added skills became clear. After eliminating the over one hundred variances that employees had found during the technical analysis, quality began to improve, cycle time was reduced, and the number of defective units was cut in half. These changes alone led to a 15 percent reduction in the center's cents-per-placement, meaning that the center had already achieved its formal goal. To the delight of both managers and employees, the improvements did not stop at 15 percent. As Steve Tracy explained, "The changes in peoples' behavior—broader skills, better communication, and more flexibility—translated into speedier troubleshooting, less downtime, and fewer defects. We found it hard to believe the numbers, but these changes had further reduced the center's production costs to a total of 25 percent!"

A RUDE AWAKENING

Despite an impressive beginning, the new design would never be fully implemented. In the months following Summer School, high-level managers had finalized HP's personal computer strategy: Grenoble would become the strategic center for all personal computer manufacturing, which meant that the Roseville Surface Mount Center would indeed be closed.

Steve Tracy felt frustrated but powerless about the decision. He explained: "We weren't privy to the discussions going on between the managers above us, and we didn't have control over the changes happening." Hendrickson provided a realistic dimension to the situation. "We don't always like the decisions that come from higher levels of the corporation," she explained. "But the scope of those decisions is corporate-wide, world-wide. And over the long haul, those decisions are in the best interest of HP employees. But that doesn't make us feel any better at the time when they're being made."

Ironically, however, the center would survive. In the preceding months, the center had taken on additional business producing boards for its next-door neighbor, the Roseville Network Division (RND), which boosted the center's production volume and allowed it to achieve greater economies of scale. (The RND was another HP division that shared the Roseville site with CPCD. It produced networking cards for computers and peripherals.) The managers of RND were pleased with the center's quality and responsiveness and were soon outsourcing a growing number and variety of boards to the center.

One day the manager of RND visited the center to find out how it was able to produce such a wide variety of high-quality boards at such low cost. The manager toured the center's production line and talked with production operators. Later, he remarked on their high levels of knowledge and flexibility. Realizing that the center would be an asset to his own division, the manager suggested to his manager that rather than close the center, it become part of RND. The higher-level managers agreed with his idea, and in August 1991 the Center was formally adopted by RND.

A Mixed Blessing

As it turned out, the Roseville Network Division's adoption of the center was a mixed blessing for the redesign effort. Although it gave the center new life, it stalled the implementation of the new design and halted the development of self-managing teams because the center's business strategy, which served as the redesign's foundation, was no longer viable. Hendrickson explained: "The design that came out of the team was tailored to a mass manufacturing environment. As part of RND, however, our new charter will be to prototype and produce low volumes and a high mix of printed circuit boards. That calls for a whole different production process—which in turn means that our new design is obsolete." In addition, the center would now have to downsize significantly because designing and prototyping boards required fewer people than manufacturing them.

Hendrickson and Tracy shared the news with the design team one afternoon in late August. As the news sank in, the design team members realized that the fears they had voiced months earlier had come true. For example, even though the center's performance had improved, business decisions regarding its future had already been made. The team members' "great ideas" would not get implemented, and some of them would not be around to see the results. Many employees said they understood the reasons behind the change in charter, but many found it deflating. "The purpose and vision statements that we spent hours creating were no longer valid," said one member. "The cornerstone of the redesign had been pulled out. The structure fell apart." The adoption became known as the "organizational earthquake of magnitude 9.5."

The design team members were especially disappointed by the change in charter because they were the ones who had championed the redesign to their peers. One member who had promoted the effort explained: "Unfortunately, a lot of what people said came true. Many said, 'I'm not going to do this self-managing redesign, it's going to be just like every other project that we start and never gets finished.' And what happened? *Exactly that.* And I was the one *defending* it, going 'No way! This is what's going to happen . . . it's going to be totally different.'"

Thus, in the months that followed, the redesign came to a disappointing standstill. Although portions of the new organizational design had been implemented—for example, the production line had been reconfigured and training classes had been established—few other aspects of the new design had moved forward. None of the planned changes designed to support self-managing teams, such as changes to the center's performance, selection, evaluation, or ranking systems, had occurred. Many supervisors still had difficulty being coaches, and much of the training designed to reinforce what employees learned in Summer School was canceled before they had a chance to acquire new skills. As a result, little progress had been made toward developing self-managing teams. One engineer said, "During Summer School, many heads were bobbing up and down like in the back of a car, but their minds were going, 'Nuh-uh.' They didn't get the agenda. The training was supposed to help them internalize the principles. But now that it's been canceled, it will be impossible to show them how to self-manage." Similarly, a design team member said, "I was deeply involved in the redesign for months. I really believed in it—I was committed to it—and I tried to make it happen. But with just a few people and one week, you can't make the same thing happen to hundreds of people. It just doesn't work. They have to experience it for themselves."

The managers and engineers who had been on the design team tried to continue developing self-managed teams by keeping both the counsels and the training running. According to the managers, however, these attempts were "steamrollered by the changes that were going on." A manager on the Business Council explained: "It became impossible to continue working toward being self-managed in this type of environment. It was obvious that the changes were going to be so massive that the best thing to do was to just focus on getting the product out, wait for the change to occur, and then accommodate it. If [the change in charter] had been an evolutionary change, we could have continued implementing the new design. But this was revolutionary. One day we're a high-volume producer of personal computer cards, and next day we are a prototype shop for network cards."

The impending downsizing curtailed any remaining effort to implement self-managing teams because employees became more concerned about their jobs than about redesigning the center. One production operator explained: "There's been so many changes in our organization lately. Right now, uppermost in most people's minds is not redesign or what they learned last year in Summer School. It's finding a job. People want to know if they're going to be here tomorrow or whether they're going to leave Roseville so they can figure out their futures. A lot of people being affected by this excess don't feel like they should wholeheartedly participate any more." Dennis Early, the center's production manager, elaborated on the incompatibility between downsizing and developing self-managing teams: "We learned it doesn't work very well to ask a team to redesign itself into a much smaller configuration. You can't get three people into a room and ask them to decide which two of them are going to leave. You can ask those three people to gather information to make a decision and propose alternatives, but ask them to make the decision for you? It isn't going to happen. At least not well. It's not going to be a positive kind of experience, it's going to be quite negative."

Despite the immense disappointment, however, many of the center's employees still believed in the redesign principles and felt optimistic about redesign's potential. Some said the impact of the redesign had not been extinguished, just temporarily obscured by the change in plans. "It wasn't wiped out, just buried," said one production operator. Many said they looked forward to the day when things would "get back to normal" and they could get back to developing themselves as a team. One production operator summed it up: "It's virtually impossible to follow [the redesign] now. But when the appropriate time arises, when we know what type of organization we will be, when those who are leaving have left, and when the line is redesigned and re–laid out in a different format—which will be at least six months down the road—the value will surface again. We'll take advantage of what we've learned and start reapplying it. Then we'll start thinking, OK, let's now start *really* becoming a self-managed team."

The Green Team

To their surprise, a small group of employees were able to apply what they learned from the redesign experience far sooner than they anticipated. To prepare the center for its new charter, management commissioned a cross-functional design team, called the Green Team, to transform the production process from one designed to manufacture boards to one designed to prototype them. Membership on the Green Team was drawn from the original design team, as well as from two counsels that had grown out of the redesign—the New Product and Process Introduction (NPPI) Counsel and the Statistical Process Control Counsel. The team also included several employees from the center's new parent organization, RND. In the fall of 1991, the Green Team began furiously redesigning the center to fit its new home in RND.

According to all accounts, the second redesign was a success. Soon after it was completed, the center was able to prototype thirty-five new boards in eight weeks, doubling managers' expectations. Much credit was given to the first redesign. Steve Tracy said of the center's employees, "They knew exactly where to look to get the information they needed—and exactly what to do next." Hendrickson explained: "The NPPI Counsel had made great progress in streamlining the new product introduction process, and the SPC Counsel ensured that quality was not sacrificed in the process, so everything was already in place." According to Dennis Early, the center was running so efficiently that "it was like having the engine all tuned up. All we had to do was drop it into the new organization. Then we had to redesign the chassis, the suspension system, and the seat for the driver!"

REFLECTIONS ON THE REDESIGN

A year later, managers and employees reflected back on the redesign and its role in the center's development. A common concern, shared by all managers, was that the redesign had been unable to keep up with the changes under way in the company's personal computer strategy. Dennis Early explained that the turbulence had caught them by surprise. "Ours was a case study of how a business objective can almost outstrip an organization's ability to change," he said. "We were aware of the need for continuing redesign and renewal even during the redesign. But we had a rather naive understanding of what that meant. What hadn't occurred to us is the possibility of needing to face change so radical that the redesign process would not be successful."

Many managers suggested that the redesign process would have to be accomplished in a shorter amount of time to keep up with HP's fast-paced computer business. One who had been on the design team said, "The organizational redesign took almost a year from start to finish, from the time we started talking about it to the time we wrapped up Summer School.[5] Well, around here, you can have two full business cycles in a year. So you cannot take a year in this environment to redesign an organization. Some of the changes that we have to make should be done in weeks." Hendrickson voiced a similar opinion. "The pace of things is too fast to think that you could ever actually survive doing redesign the way we did it in the Surface Mount Center," she said, "because by the time you start and stop it, the world is different. Heck, by the time we got down to implementing the proposal, if we had done a business analysis again, we would have had a 180 degree different scenario." She continued, questioning the traditional approach to STS redesign: "I'd like to sit down and have a philosophical discussion with the work redesign theorists who espouse the kind of structured, linear process—first you form the steering committee, then the design team, then do the business analysis, then the technical analysis, etc. . . . because if you start down the path that way, you may get no farther than a block before something changes and you have to adapt again." She added that she had recently advised a group of engineers in

5. Henson and other managers on the steering committee had begun talking about redesigning the center in mid-1990, several months before the design team was formed in December of that year.

another division which was just starting a redesign that if they could not finish their first iteration of the analysis and design process in two or three months, they were taking "way too long."

The other critical issue, managers maintained, was that the center did not have control over its charter. Dennis Early explained: "You can change three things. First, you can change your business—the way you generate revenue streams and the way you manage your money in the organization. Or you can change the technology. Or you can change the organization. As we looked around at what needed to be changed, we saw a business threat, but we couldn't change our charter by ourselves. We didn't see a technological solution. So the only thing left for us to change was the organization."

Steve Tracy suggested that the redesign should have been initiated at the level where the division's business strategy was formed. "We started in production as the core," he explained. "You need to start from the top. We should have started with business as the core and considered production, manufacturing, engineering, and marketing as components. If we had done that it would have been more clear, early on, what the needed changes were and how to support them. If you really want to redesign an organization for empowerment and self-management, the entire organization has to make that decision at the business level. It's got to be high enough so if the business shifts, everybody who is involved is aware of what is going on and is able to shift with it." Tracy surmised, however, that initiating redesign at the division level would be difficult because not all higher-level managers agreed with the redesign philosophy of shifting authority downward. He explained: "Redesign is not yet a value at higher levels of management. There's still a paradigm shirt—a value shift—that has to happen. The idea of a self-empowered workforce is one of the most difficult parts of the whole redesign concept to put into practice. It's very difficult for our upper managers to relinquish control. I think there may be some rugged individualist control needs up there that haven't shifted yet. If you're going to design your business around processes and provide decision-making resources for people at lower levels, you have to be willing to allow that to happen. But that's not just a Hewlett-Packard problem, that's an American problem. Control is a very important American management value and it's difficult for managers to give up."

Despite concerns about the length of the redesign and where it had been started, managers agreed on its value—the most obvious evidence being that it had saved the center's life. "It saved our bacon," said Dennis Early. "It was the only reason we weren't vaporized." The value of the redesign, managers and employees agreed, had come not from the design itself but from the numerous activities undertaken in the process of creating it. Although self-managing teams had never been realized, the center's employees had become more knowledgeable, committed, and flexible. Dennis Early explained: "Having the team go out and do a business, technical, and organizational analysis. Those activities, and the learning that came from them, changed the way a substantial population out there perceived their individual jobs. That's what created the lasting value." Another manager added, "Working next to managers and engineers, learning about the business side of the center, and redesigning their own organization really dethreatened and deintimidated folks."

Some managers suggested that redesign should be considered a continuous process rather than a onetime event. Hendrickson said: "I think we've viewed this as a onetime effort. We did it and we finished it and that's it. If we were to maintain the discipline and maintain the work redesign mentality, we could keep up with that pace of change. If you're really going to use redesign as a total quality management mechanism to examine everything, improve yourself, and deepen your understanding of your customers' needs, and so on out through the model, then you'd better do redesign quickly and view it as a cyclical process. You can't think of it as a project that you start and stop, and now you're done. The question really becomes, how do you design in continuous design?"

Redesign may become a continuous event, another manager explained, as the learning that employees gain through the redesign experience becomes internalized. He said: "I don't think the amount of time the redesign took was a weakness. It's hard to separate out, but I think a lot of that [time] was organizational learning, or teaching the organization how to learn, versus doing a redesign. It could be that if we went back now and did another redesign in production we could get it done in weeks."

Managers agreed that the value of the first redesign had carried over to the second one. Steve Tracy said, "Greater flexibility on the part of our people was a tangible outcome of the first redesign that contributed to the center's successful transition from a manufacturing to a prototype shop." Hendrickson noted, "The folks who went through the redesign are more adaptable and resilient than their peers. You could see their maturity in dealing with the transition. Some of that is because of the turbulent environment they've been in, but a lot of it is due to the redesign. I can't imagine how we would have done the second redesign had we not done the first."

7 • THE SANTA CLARA DIVISION REDESIGN

The Santa Clara Division, established in 1961, is HP's second oldest division. It is also one of twenty in HP's Test and Measurement Group. For almost thirty years, the division designed and built high-tech, general-purpose test and measurement electronic instruments. It's atomic clocks, driven by the oscillations of a cesium atom, lose no more than one second every million years and are used to define the world's time standard. Laser interferometers and frequency counters set similarly high standards for measuring motion and frequency. The Santa Clara Division became a major supplier for the defense industry because of the excellence of its products, and during the Cold War years, it enjoyed unprecedented sales to such prime aerospace contractors as McDonnell Douglas and Hughes Aircraft. With its dominant position in test and measurement markets, the division had few competitors, and it grew steadily. By the mid-1980s, its revenue stood at an all-time high and its workforce had reached sixteen hundred.

Within the next few years, changes in the external environment halted the division's growth. The most significant change was a decline in the aerospace defense industry, the division's largest customer base that had been, according to division manager Marty Neil, the "wind in our sails." By the early 1990s, cutbacks in government defense spending that followed the end of the Cold War had reduced the division's largest business segment to half its original size.

The test and measurement market had also changed. Customers were shifting from analog to digital equipment, and computer-aided engineering was proliferating. Both changes portended the decline of the stand-alone, off-the-shelf test and measurement equipment that had made Santa Clara famous. Computer-aided engineering could now produce designs of such high quality that they never required testing. The quality revolution also forced HP's manufacturing customers to improve their production techniques. As their quality improved, they realized that testing added unnecessary costs to production and that much of it could be eliminated.

Along with the decline in defense spending and shifts in technology, the competition for the remaining test and measurement markets became increasingly fierce. By the late 1980s the test and measurement industry had fragmented into many niche businesses and specialized products, and the number of suppliers grew into thousands. Aggressive competitors also began tailoring products to their customers' demands for complete, integrated solutions to their problems, rather than stand-alone, general-purpose boxes that simply provided data.

By 1992, these changes had taken their toll on the Santa Clara Division. Its revenue had been cut in half, and one thousand of its sixteen hundred employees had left in a series of painful downsizings. Unless the division was able to find new customers and businesses, it would either be shut down or merged with an existing HP division.

ORIGIN OF THE REDESIGN

In November 1991, Marty Neil took over the Santa Clara Division in hopes of restoring its competitiveness. Neil, an engineer with a background in marketing, felt pressure from his boss, who headed the Electronic Instruments Group, to find a new strategy for the division's growth. He knew that reversing its dire situation would require radical steps and that it would have to be transformed if it were to survive.

In the spring of 1992, Bob Shultz joined the division as its new controller. He came from HP's Eastern Sales Region, where he had served as a sponsor and steering committee member for a nonlinear work redesign project. Shultz suggested taking an STS approach to redesigning the division because, as he explained, "It's how I'd like to be managed." He recalled: "I saw it as the best way to break the logjam, the historical inertia, and change the values and culture of the division to be more focused on customers' needs."

Neil agreed with Shultz's reasoning and, in May 1992, embarked on what would become a three-year redesign effort to transform the division. As a first step, he would charter a cross-functional team of managers who would conduct an accelerated, ten-week "macro-level" redesign effort to diagnose the division's problems. Later, Neil would sponsor a "micro-level redesign" that would be conducted by two additional teams over the course of a year: a new product development (NPD) team that would reengineer the new product development process and a transition team that would align the inside of the organization with the division's new values and business strategy.

THE MACRO-LEVEL REDESIGN

The macro redesign was conducted between June and August 1992. While it followed STS methodology, the redesign was to be high-level and abbreviated and aimed at broad scope rather than depth.[1] The design team consisted of managers from R&D, marketing, manufacturing, materials, finance, and personnel. First, the team conducted a brief analysis of the division's business situation by reviewing with Neil the outcome of the 1992 Business Strategy Review (BSR), an annual planning document for group-sector management used to describe the division's business strategy for the coming three- to five-year period. As the team members suspected, the division had failed to meet its projected revenue targets for the past several years. To their amazement, they also learned that the division had the lowest-order growth and poorest return on investments (ROI) of any division in Test and Measurement.

Next, the team identified the division's strengths and weaknesses that were influencing its business performance. The division's strengths, the team concluded, were that it had an excellent market position, was highly capable of developing new technology, and had access to some of the most talented engineers in the world. The division also enjoyed an excellent reputation among its customers. Among its weaknesses, the design team found that though it was a leader in the test and measurement industry, this market was declining. The division also had a poor history of choosing profitable businesses and had consistently chosen projects that broke new ground technologically but had poor ROIs. The division's decision-making process was also inefficient because of a dysfunctional relationship between the top management staff and cross-functional business teams. Finally, the division's product development cycles were far too long.

Once the design team understood the division's dire business situation, it concluded that the overarching problem was that the division had been slow to recognize changes in its business environment and consequently had failed to adapt. "Once we realized that," said Jenny Brandemuehl, who would lead the division's transition, "the next—and most difficult—question to answer was, Why had we been so slow to change? *Why hadn't we seen the writing on the wall?*"

The answer to this question came from the design team's social analysis, which revealed that the division's behavior was rooted in its inward orientation. The business environment had been changing for almost six years,

---

1. I began research at the division in February 1993, after the macro redesign team had completed its work. This account of the micro redesign, therefore, was reconstructed from peoples' memories and from documents and thus does not have the same rich detail as later sections.

Conclusion

but the division had been blinded by its focus on technology. This problem, Neil explained, had been masked by good business. "We grew 15 percent a year from the mid-'60s to the late '80s. After more than twenty years of growth, we had little reason to question our charter, which was given to us by our founders. So we continued aiming all our effort at traditional markets, not growth areas. Despite our declining market, we continued to invest heavily in R&D and developed new technologies even though we were getting the lowest returns on our investments of any division in HP's test and measurement business. When our customers began to disappear, we continued like nothing had changed. So the handwriting was on the wall for some time. We were just slow to read it. We were fat, dumb, and happy within the walls of our division."

The division had little reason to look outside its walls because its engineers were their own best customers, often using the very products they built (e.g., oscillators and counters) in their daily work to create new products. They had only to look to their peers at the next bench for new ideas—a phenomenon engineers called the "next bench syndrome." Even when in separate divisions, engineers created what Neil called a "virtual" next bench in their minds. They imagined what their customers wanted and, convinced that they were correct, focused their attention on designing the most technologically advanced products possible. According to Neil, "We were introverted, absorbed in science and technology to the extent that nothing else existed. We were called the 'Science Fair' Division by the field sales organization because we had a reputation for loving any new technology that came along. It wasn't meant as a compliment, but we took it as one!"

Even if the division had been more in tune with its changing environment, it could not have responded because of its organizational structure. According to Neil, "Not only were we in the wrong businesses, but we had the wrong organization!" Like most large organizations, the division was structured around functions such as R&D, marketing, manufacturing, and finance. This structure would have worked well if the division had one business because Neil's management staff, which consisted of the top managers of each of the functional areas, would work as the business team to run the business. The diversity and complexity of the division's businesses, however, caused it to form multifunction business teams made up of three or four mid-level managers from R&D, marketing, and manufacturing that were chartered to run the businesses by the management staff. The business teams had the knowledge to make decisions, but they did not have the power. The management staff, in turn, had the authority to make decisions but frequently wanted more information than the business teams provided. As a result, the management staff would postpone business decisions and ask the business teams to "get more data" (a pattern that Neil called "decision constipation"). Or, decisions were made that favored the division's functions, rather than its businesses. As a result, products were often late to market, and optimistic sales forecasts were rarely realized.

The design team also conducted a technical analysis by identifying and analyzing the division's four core cross-functional processes: market choice (the process of choosing markets to enter), product choice (the process of choosing technologies to pursue), new product development (the process of developing new products), and manufacturing. The design team members interviewed individuals in the division who were most knowledgeable about these processes to learn how well they worked.[2] They found that two of the division's four core processes—market choice and new product development—were the key reasons behind its dismal returns from its investments in new products. In fact, the team realized that because the division had been so technology-driven and had never needed to look for customers, it did not even really *have* a market choice process. The new product development process, in turn, was enormously complex and far too slow. By the time products were finally released, they were typically way over budget and far behind schedule.

Finally, the design team identified two main characteristics that the division would have to acquire to survive and grow. First, it would have to become highly responsive to customers' needs and look to them in developing new products. Second, the division's employees would have to become more empowered and be given the knowledge and authority to make decisions quickly, on their own.

After ten weeks of analyses, the design team gave its proposal to the steering committee in August 1992. The overarching recommendation was that the division replace its functional structure with a flatter matrix structure, organized by businesses called "customer segments" (see Figure 6). The division's three existing businesses would be consolidated into two. The first customer segment would be called Timing Solutions for Communications (TSC) and include the cesium clock and frequency counter businesses. The second would be called Precision Motion Control (PMC) and consist of the laser interferometer business. Each new customer segment

2. Because traditional sociotechnical systems' technical tools were unsuitable for the nonlinear, "knowledge" nature of processes such as new product development, for their technical analysis the macro team used the interrelationship and process mapping tools provided by the Rummler-Brache group based on Geary Rummler and Alan Brache's book *Improving Performance: How to Manage the White Space on the Organization Chart* (San Francisco: Jossey-Bass, 1990).

would be run by new business teams that would have both the knowledge *and* the authority to make decisions. Dismantling the functional organization and reorganizing the division around businesses, the design team reasoned, would also remove the functional barriers and create "blended jobs" that would require crossover between functions. It would require, for example, that R&D engineers devote more attention to marketing, selling, and interfacing with customers. This new structure would also remove managers' tendency to make decisions that optimized the R&D, marketing, and manufacturing functions at the expense of the business.

Heading each new customer segment would be new "customer segment" managers (CSMs) who would be responsible for the profitability, loss, and growth of an entire business segment.[3] Working with their business teams, the CSMs would develop a vision for the future of their business segments and a plan to lead them there. The design team reasoned that the CSMs could not possibly develop such an externally focused vision while sitting in the division; such vision could come only while sitting with the customer. Therefore, the CSM's job would be primarily what the team called an "outside job." The CSMs would be expected to spend between one-third to one-half of their time outside the division with customers, field engineers, and potential business partners.

The team also recommended merging the support parts of the former R&D, marketing, and quality assurance functions into a new entity called New Product and Process Services (NPPS), which would service the customer segments. Combining the former R&D and marketing functions, Neil hoped, would also encourage engineers to become more flexible and work across functional boundaries. The establishment of NPPS represented the division's attempt to shorten its new product development process. The NPPS manager would head the departments that supported the new product development process (PC layout, industrial design, mechanical and quality engineering, technical information systems, labstock, new product support, marketing communication, and graphics). If NPPS was unable to meet the needs of the businesses, the CSMs had the authority to outsource the services required—a first for the division, which historically placed great value on producing every aspect of the product in-house. The manufacturing organization, for the time being, would remain unchanged, except that it would be renamed Order Fulfillment to reflect the division's new focus on processes as opposed to functions. Finally, the team recom-

3. The customer segment manager was given this name, rather than being called a business manager, to emphasize the division's dependence on finding new customers before new businesses could be established.

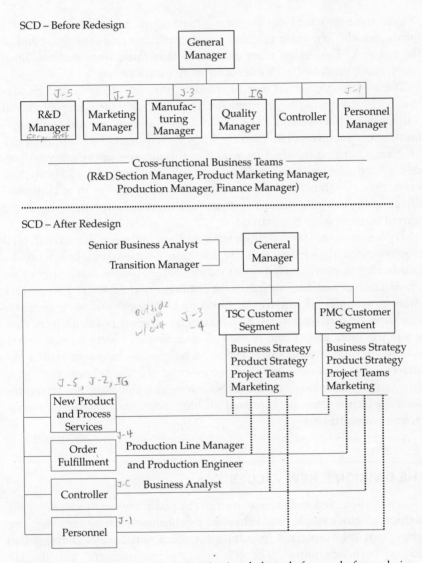

Figure 6. Santa Clara Division organizational chart, before and after redesign

mended that Jenny Brandemuehl, the former personnel manager, be hired for eighteen months as transition manager.

While the design team analyzed all four of the division's core processes, they recommended that the redesign focus on two: the market choice process, which would have to be created, and the new product development process, which was most in need of improvement. Brandemuehl explained:

"Given the urgency of our business situation, we had to make improvements quickly. We knew that our burning platform was the front end of the business. The design team discovered that those were our two most problematic processes, so we went to work on those first."

The most controversial part of the design team's recommendation was that the restructuring begin immediately, even before new customers and businesses had been found. The design team reasoned that although organizational structure might account for only 20 percent of the division's problem, changing its structure would enable changes in the other 80 percent of the problem—the division's culture—to begin. In addition, Neil knew that the transformation from a technology-driven to a customer-driven culture would require a massive cultural change that should be started sooner rather than later.

To demonstrate his commitment to pushing authority downward, Neil recommended that individuals for the new positions be chosen not by him but by employees. Neil informed employees that he was going to set up selection committees to interview candidates, and he asked employees either to volunteer themselves or someone else they would want to represent them on the committees. Candidates for the new positions were chosen in the same way. Once the selection committees were formed, members learned behavioral interviewing techniques to help standardize the interviewing process. After they interviewed the candidates, they gave their recommendations to Neil. Neil reserved the right to reject the teams' selections, but he approved all four individuals chosen by the selection committees.

THE DIVISION'S NEW VALUES

In late 1992 Neil and his new staff developed a new set of values for the division to guide employees' behavior. Establishing clear values, Neil reasoned, would be especially important because a new business strategy had not yet been determined. The new values were consistent with the HP Way, but they were personalized to emphasize the behaviors that the division would have to adopt to survive in its new environment (see Figure 7). For instance, in addition to stressing the traditional values inherent in the HP Way such as trust, respect, and integrity in working relationships, the new values emphasized the need for employees to have a greater sense of urgency and to become more customer-focused. They also stressed the need for employees to meet their commitments (project deadlines), to become more versatile and take on a wider variety of tasks, and to be externally focused and able to identify new business opportunities.

Our people
- We value broadly skilled, versatile people who can contribute to many parts of the organization.
- We value creative people with the initiative to drive breakthroughs and teach the rest of us from their successes and failures.
- We value externally focused people with the ability to sense business opportunities and match the needs of our customers with innovative products.
- We value continuous learning and development because our people are our only sustainable competitive advantage.

Our customers
- We value total dedication to customer satisfaction for the long-term benefits of each customer relationship.
- We value total customer involvement in all aspects of our business: customers drive our decisions, our processes, and are the reason for our organization's existence.
- We value customer segment–focused solutions for the clarity of direction and competitive advantage they provide.

Our business
- We value meeting commitments for the freedom of action it provides; we value results, not just activity.
- We value decisiveness and a sense of urgency for the increased effectiveness they bring to everything we do.

Our working relationships
- We value integrity and candor.
- We value teamwork and diversity for the multiplying effect it provides to individual efforts.
- We value winning for the energy, joy, and enthusiasm it creates through validating our ability to meet customer needs better than our competitors.
- We value trust and respect for every individual.

Figure 7. Santa Clara Division values

FISCAL YEAR 1993 OBJECTIVES

In late 1992, Neil and his staff developed two major multi-year objectives, known as "Hoshins," for the 1993 fiscal year which would serve as the foundation for the second stage of the redesign. The first objective (Hoshin 2.0), was to improve, by fivefold, the division's returns on its investments in new products so as to achieve double-digit yearly growth in net profit by 1997. In the long run, the division aimed to become a growing supplier of test and measurement solutions by focusing on specific customer segments. Neil and his staff set forth specific strategies to achieve this objective. First, the division would expand and redefine its business charters. Second, it would improve its method for predicting projects' rate of return and for selecting projects that would yield high rates of return. Third, the division would reduce the cost of getting new products to market by reengineering the new product development process. Fourth, the division would adopt a new strategy called "SDBS," which stands for "Sell-Design-Build-Support," under which products would be designed and built only *after* the product ideas were sold to customers. Finally, the division would invest only in its core capabilities and outsource any remaining activities to low-cost suppliers.

The second objective (Hoshin 3.0) was to align the division's internal systems and practices with its business strategies (once found) and values. The overall goal of this objective was to become HP's leading example of a "bottom-up, customer-driven" organization whose employees exhibited high levels of leadership and initiative. Neil set forth specific strategies to achieve this objective. First, a transition team would be formed to identify and propose changes to the division's structure and culture to bring them into alignment with its values. Second, decision-making responsibility would be placed at the lowest levels possible. Third, management would create incentives for engineers to meet project commitment dates. Fourth, opportunities would be created for employees to develop the skills and behaviors needed to create the ability to adapt to constant change. Finally, training would be provided on demand so that employees could apply it immediately. If necessary, subject matter experts would be called in to help employees learn the skills needed to make the transition.

THE NEW BUSINESS

In the first few months of 1993, with the division's new structure in place, Neil and his new staff aggressively conducted market investigations to find a new business that would enable the division to grow. In April of that year, they decided on a new division charter. The division would maintain its test and measurement business but pin its future growth on the communications industry. The new business would be called "Synchronization for Communications," or "Sync" for short. As explained by Murli Thirumale, the CSM of the new customer segment, Sync would lead the division into the information age by solving the increasing problems of the growing communications infrastructure. "As the information superhighway becomes a reality," Thirumale explained, "digital data will be transferred over wire and through air at increasingly higher speeds, greater volumes, and wider bandwidths. The communication systems at each end of the data transfer will have to be synchronized to prevent data from being lost in the transmission. An analogy is Coke bottles traveling through a factory on conveyer belts; unless the conveyer belts and all the other equipment operate at the same rate, you'll have Coke bottles dropping on the floor. Synchronizing communication systems would prevent the loss of financial data as it is transferred from the New York to the Japan stock exchange, errors in facsimile outputs, or 'garbage' on computer terminals in wire transmissions. In wireless communications, synchronization would eliminate the pops and glitches that are heard on a cellular car phone as one drives from the vicinity of one wireless baystation to another. It would also enable the wireless transfer of higher-bandwidth data such as digitized documents or video."

Thirumale's strategy was to create a universal time standard, or what he called a "ubiquitous timing utility," for the communications industry. The actual timekeeping device would be called an HP "SmartClock" that would be created by marrying two already existing technologies (a counter and a quartz oscillator). By taking advantage of the accurate timing provided by the Global Positioning System (GPS), the SmarkClock would provide reliable, cesium-quality time for 10 percent of the cost. This technology would have tremendous applications in the communications industry, especially given the predicted explosive growth of the communications infrastructure in the United States, as well as in China and other developing nations.

Sync was a radical departure from the division's traditional business. For the first time, the division would build products that would be used for purposes other than test and measurement. Thirumale explained: "Our test and measurement business was analogous to the hammer that hits the table to test its sturdiness. Sync is like building the table's legs." The division aimed to become the leading supplier of timing modules and synchronization solutions for the wireless and telecommunications industries by the end of the 1997 fiscal year.

Managers and engineers had high hopes for Sync. The first business decision to come out of the new organizational structure, Sync had the potential to reverse the division's track record of poor business decisions and restore its economic vitality. Yet entering a brand new business, especially one in which the division had little experience, was risky, and it would take a substantial investment of time and resources. As one engineer explained, "It takes a lot of legwork to find out about markets you've never been in before." Some engineers feared that managers would become impatient and exit the business prematurely before it had a chance to become profitable—a tendency engineers called the "grand-slam" mentality.

One engineer explained: "There is a high cost to getting in. It'll be tough to generate the funding we'll need to sustain us while we work our way in. We're expecting that we're going to be able to go out and jump into a new business and within a year to be reaping great profits. It won't happen that fast. It will take a long, painful period of time."

THE MICRO-LEVEL REDESIGN

In January 1993, as the skeleton of the new division was being implemented, Neil kicked off the second stage of the redesign. The goal of this micro redesign was to achieve the two 1993 fiscal year objectives. The micro redesign was conducted by two separate teams, the new product development (NPD) team and the transition team, which ran in parallel between January and August 1993. The NPD team took on the task of reengineering the new product development process to help improve the division's ROI, while the transition team was charged with aligning the division's structure, systems, culture, and management practices with its new values. Although Neil and Brandemuehl knew that separating the analyses could limit the integration of the teams' findings, they decided to split up the work because there was not enough time to do the analyses sequentially. In an effort to achieve as much crossover as possible, two individuals served as members of both teams, and the teams made efforts to keep abreast of each other's activities and findings.

The NPD team met for the first time in January 1993 and would meet every other week, for approximately four hours, for six months. The ten-member cross-functional team consisted of five engineers (from R&D and marketing), one production operator from manufacturing, three managers, and one person from finance. As a first step, the NPD team reviewed a project called "6X" that had failed to meet its deadline. Named after an English beer that the engineers were drinking when they invented it, 6X was a time interval analyzer used to test products in the exploding wireless industry. The goal of the project was to meet a six-month time-to-market, but the product was nine months late reaching customers' hands. (Ironically, the project was not considered a total failure because it did not miss its market window; the wireless market projections were also nine months off.)

Although project reviews, called "postpartums" were typical at the division, they were usually conducted by managers, and their findings were rarely disseminated. Instead, Brandemuehl decided to have engineers on the NPD team conduct the postpartum to teach them how to look for the technical as well as the social factors that contributed to projects' cost and schedule overruns.

The major finding from the 6X postpartum was that the project was over budget and over schedule by a factor of two. In other words, the product had taken twice as long and had cost twice as much to develop and build than originally planned. Ironically, these overruns were caused mainly by cultural or structural factors rather than technical factors. For example, the engineers found a lack of "ownership" for the project, meaning that no one person (or team) had been held accountable for getting the 6X product to market on time. None of the R&D engineers who had worked on the project were the least concerned about missing the deadline—in fact, they did not even know when the deadline was. Eager to get the project funded, they had given their managers overly optimistic time lines that they knew managers wanted to hear. In addition, while engineers knew that outsourcing certain services such as the PC layout process (the process of laying out printed circuits onto a board) would have saved time and money, they had not suggested it because they knew it would violate the division's tradition of keeping every step in the new product development process in-house.

After reviewing the revealing findings of the 6X postpartum, engineers on the NPD team were curious as to how representative they were of other projects in the division. To find out, they collected actual and estimated cost, sales volume, and completion dates for all projects that had been completed by the division within the last two years. After comparing the actual versus estimated figures for these measures, they found that most projects, like the 6X, had been over budget by a factor of two. Budget overruns were found to be correlated with schedule overruns in 90 percent of the cases. Schedule overruns, the NPD team reasoned, led to budget overruns because even when projects were far behind schedule, they were rarely canceled. Meanwhile, engineers who were determined to bring the technology to fruition continued working on them, accumulating additional costs. Sales volumes, in addition, were found to be on average half as large as expected. Finally, the team found that, like the 6X project, no one was held accountable for projects being over cost and over budget.

To prepare to reengineer the NPD process, engineers on the NPD team interviewed other engineers and managers to document exactly how the new product development process worked. Using business process reengineering tools, they created a map that illustrated the process by which products were defined, developed, built, evaluated, and delivered to the customer (see Figure 8). Their findings revealed problems in three phases of the new product development process: the PC layout phase, the project specification phase, and software and hardware reuse. First, they found that the PC layout process was not competitive and could be obtained at a lower cost from outside vendors. Second, they found that while product

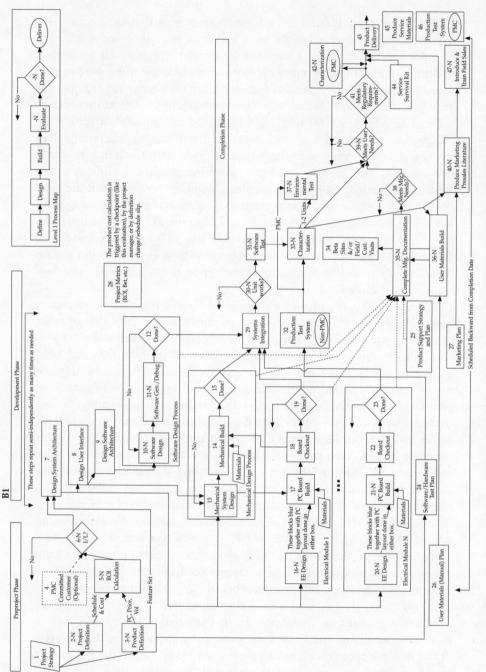

Figure 8. Santa Clara Division new product development process map (level 2)

ideas were supposed to exit the product specification phase fully defined and specified, instead they were being approved by managers even though product definitions "varied all over the place." This lack of project definitions typically led to errors in developing new product prototypes. Finally, they found that because of the division's focus on invention, product designs, software, and hardware were being used only once, rather than being leveraged and reused to save additional resources.

The NPD team also found a range of hidden beliefs—on the part of both managers and engineers—that contributed to project cost and schedule overruns. For instance, they found that managers typically favored and funded high-profile, potentially lucrative products called "grand slams" that required heavy investments but often failed to sell over those based on incremental improvements on existing products that promised slow but steady growth, otherwise known as "base hits." They also found that management tended to reward problem solving, or "firefighting," rather than preventing problems in the first place. The NPD team also found that although marketing engineers viewed delays in the R&D process as periods of wasted time, most R&D engineers considered them "normal and acceptable" and had little incentive to meet project deadlines. R&D engineers saw R&D as a creative and unpredictable process that was impossible to standardize. "I cannot invent on a schedule" was a familiar refrain. R&D engineers considered any attempt to predict the new product development process as "confining." To avoid feeling pressured when managers inevitably asked them to shorten their cycle time, engineers had learned to "fudge the numbers" and build extra time into project schedules. At the opposite extreme, when engineers were eager to get projects funded, they would give managers unrealistic deadlines to make the project seem more attractive. They knew the deadline could not possibly be met, but they also knew there were no consequences for delays.

Mark Allen, the new manager of NPPS and the leader of the NPD team, viewed the findings from the team's investigation of actual versus estimated project measures as proof that the new product development cycle could be standardized. "All engineers have to do is multiply their estimates by two. Everyone can compute that," he said jokingly. Having gathered and analyzed the data themselves, the engineers on the team were forced to agree—but only partially. One engineer explained:

In our culture, engineers tend to say, 'What I do is R&D. I can't tell you how long it will take to invent something.' But I learned from our findings is that there is 'R,' for research, and 'D,' for development. Most people blur those together. R isn't *supposed* to be predictable. You can't say, 'Today I'm going to invent something.' That's random. You simply cannot predict how long it will take to invent technology out of thin air. But then there's development. After the idea has been created it's just a matter of developing the circuits, the schematics, putting the circuits on a PC board, testing the product . . . that's all development and is somewhat predictable. Yes, things will go wrong because you've never done it before. That's why it's development, not production. But we found that the delays in the product development process are, for the most part, systematic. So you can standardize the development part but not the research.

In April 1993 the second, transition team was formed to assess the organizational changes needed to align the division's structure, culture, and practices with its values (Hoshin 3.0). Brandemuehl circulated a flyer that read, "We need volunteers to help us transform the Santa Clara Division!" to solicit members. The outcome was a twelve-member team made up of seven engineers, four managers, and the senior business analyst. The team met for approximately ten hours per week (six more than originally planned) for three months.

Neil attended the transition team's kickoff meeting in early April to explain why the division needed to change and what the team's role would be. "We as a division have to modify and change our direction substantially," he said.

For the past six months, we've been thinking of change as two interrelated transitions. The first is in our philosophy of doing business. The second is how we carry business out and function as an organization. We need to change from being internally focused to externally focused. Why? Because now there's a negative demand for our test and measurement products which will not change. Three environmental shifts have occurred: (1) the decline in aerospace and defense spending; (2) technological changes—the shift from analog to digital, as well as the quality movement and elimination of the need to test; and (3) an increase in the number of companies who are competing in our markets. Santa Clara is a classic test and measurement division, and we're in for a prolonged industry shakeout till the year 2000. The problem is, we're riding the classic test and measurement bandwagon, which will be difficult for us. We need to widen our business charter and our playing field. We also need to change our focus from extending our technology charters to picking customer segments.

Neil then explained the transition team's role. "I'm assuming you're here because you care deeply about the future of the division," he said. "Your job is to figure out how to align the organization with our new values. My hope is that you would come up with a proposal as to how to develop an organization that is customer-driven and built around initiative and personal leadership." Neil explained that his staff would serve as the transition team's steering committee, and it would guide and sanction the team's proposed changes. "Go to it," he said, concluding his talk. "And remember . . . nothing is off limits with regard to your recommendations."

In part because of the enormity of their task, the team got off to a slow, frustrating start. It soon became clear that engineers did not fully understand the concept of "aligning the division with its values." The larger problem, however, was that the steering committee began to worry that the charter it had given the team was too broad, and it tried several times to make it more narrow. As a result, for the first month the team's charter changed almost weekly. First, the steering committee suggested that the team focus only on the social aspects of the new product development process and leave structural issues for a later date. A week later, after the CSM for lasers asked that his organization be excluded from the redesign (because he felt it worked well already), the micro team found that they were to focus only on the new TSC customer segment. Although the team members tried to be patient, they soon showed signs of frustration. For several weeks upon entering their meetings they quipped, "*What's* our objective *today?*"

The steering committee's ambivalence surfaced most poignantly at a strategic retreat for managers held in Half Moon Bay, when Neil introduced and advocated to his staff a new role he labeled "program leader." Unlike project leaders, these new program leaders would be responsible for an entire business (or family of related products), and program teams would be held accountable for financial results. After getting over their initial resistance to being "handed" the concept, Neil's staff began discussing the degree of control, or veto power, they should give to the transition team over the idea. The following exchange between the members of the management staff revealed their difficulty with the notion of empowerment:

Neil (division manager):	Do we propose the program leader idea to the transition team and see what they think, or do we tell them we've done it?
Controller:	We could pilot the idea with them . . . see what they think.
Neil:	What if they say they don't like it?
Financial analyst:	(half-joking) Tell them we're doing it anyway!
Thirumale (manager of Sync):	But we can't tell them what to do . . . that's not *empowering*.
Controller:	Maybe they could *evaluate* the idea.

Manager of lasers:	I'm not so sure the program leader idea should be a subject of the transition team in the first place.
Thirumale:	This empowerment stuff is the pits!

A week later, back at the site, Neil introduced the program leader concept to the transition team as a "working hypothesis." Initially, many of the engineers on the transition team did not understand the program leader concept and resented being "handed the right answer." Several engineers demanded, "How do they know the program leader is the ideal way to go?" Others asked, "How is it different from a project manager?" and "Isn't it just creating another layer of management?" Several complained: "If Marty really believed in self-directed work teams, he wouldn't have shoved the program leader at us. Talk about a disconnect . . . I think they need some training in how to be a better steering committee." Later, one engineer on the team summarized the situation: "We didn't understand the responsibility we were given, which on top of that kept changing. Management didn't bracket their line of authority or set the range of expectations for us. They could have made it clearer by saying, 'It's our job to make decisions about and implement management structures, including the program leader idea. Your job as the transition team is to figure out how things can work below management structures to the best advantage of the company.'"

In the ensuing weeks, the frustration and resentment felt by the transition team members were defused through repeated visits by Neil and Thirumale, who apologized for the steering committee's ambivalence and explained the reasoning behind the program leader concept. During one meeting Thirumale told the team, "I need to admit a few things. If I were in your shoes, I'd be confused as heck, just like you guys are. The staff screwed up." In turn, Neil explained that the steering committee wanted the transition team to come up with the program leader concept but did so itself out of a sense of urgency to generate new business as soon as possible. He explained how this would work: "The purpose of the program leader concept is to push responsibility down to the level of the team so that entire teams, rather than one person, are concerned about the long-term viability of the business. I simply want the project teams to be far broader in what they're worried about. Instead of saying, 'Here's your two-year project, go do it,' we'll be saying to them, 'Here are the financials and the direction of the business. Give us the best return you can, and tell us where to invest.' That way the program leaders and CSMs can focus on generating new business."

After several weeks the steering committee clarified the transition team's charter. It would be responsible for designing a new internal structure for the division that would encourage engineers to work as self-managing teams taking on more responsibility for the business and accountability for results—all the while ensuring that their jobs remained satisfying. Thus management had decided on the top-level structure of the organization (which included program leaders), and the transition team would design everything below.

Despite the clarification of their charter, many transition team members remained skeptical about Neil's strategy of reorganizing the division before a tangible business strategy was in place. (Sync was still in the idea stage, and no actual customers had yet been found.) Several engineers on the transition team admitted that they had agreed to join the team out of a sense of "civic duty," not because they were convinced of the need for the redesign. One engineer explained: "Many of us wonder: Is organizational redesign really what the division should be focusing on? Is it really the answer to the division's problems? Many of us think not and that we shouldn't be spending time on this now. We should be figuring out what we are going to build, what our product line is going to be. If management feels that reorganizations are needed, they should be more of a secondary, long-term thing."

A deeper reason for engineers' concern, however, was their resistance to becoming customer-driven. The new customer focus was most apparent in the division's new SDBS, or "Sell-Design-Build-Support" strategy. Engineers would work with customers to determine their needs and then develop an idea for a product. Only after customers committed themselves to buy the finished product could it be designed and built.

The SDBS strategy was profoundly different from the HP norm: "DBSS," or "Design-Build-Sell-Support." One engineer on the team described how it used to be: "It's been technology-driven. We, the creative people in this company, think of the products to make. We'd think they're so neat that when we put them out on the marketplace they would sell like hotcakes. In many cases it has worked out that way. That's what you have to do if you're going to be a leader and a driver in this market. *You* define what the standards are. Then everybody jumps in place to conform to you because you're the market leader. You got there by thinking of something the customer didn't even know he needed, or wanted. When they saw it, they said, 'This is great! I'm sure glad you thought of it!' Then everybody and his friends start using it, and there you go."

Engineers anticipated that it would be tremendously difficult for them to listen to customers because the old way of working was extremely gratifying—and it was the way they had been taught to work. One engineer explained: "Making the transition from a technology-driven company to a customer-driven one will be very difficult for us. The longer you've been here, the harder it will be to change because that's not the way we were taught to think right from college. I was technology-driven . . . I remember what it felt like to come up with the seed idea. I'd brainstorm with the guy sitting next to me, and suddenly we'd come up with a neat new product! That's why SDBS is going to be so hard to implement. We've done it the old way so long."

Many engineers found it difficult to accept the notion that "the customer is king." One manager said, "The biggest problem is getting people to look outward and to identify and accept that customer needs are based on what customers tell us, not on what *we* think a customer wants." Another engineer noted: "It's hard for many engineers to make the transition. When an engineer gets an 'ah-ha,' it's very subjective and gratifying, and it's impossible for him to hear that a customer doesn't want it. Some engineers literally have to be hit over the head with a baseball bat to hear anything, and that rigidity tends to worsen with age."

Not only was the old way of working inherently gratifying, R&D engineers believed it was successful. One engineer explained: "We'd be allowed to work on ideas that had no definite marketplace yet. We were determined to make whatever we were working on the *best* of this thing that we could make. We did it, and then oftentimes they would find an application for it. That's why HP has the reputation as the best, highest-quality, leading-edge instrument company in the world."

Many engineers also feared that the customer focus would lead to the loss of technology and eventually to the division's demise. One said, "If we only do stuff the customer is interested in, we'll lose our expertise in technology and the division will go out of business." Others predicted that if forced to become customer-focused, the best engineers would leave. One engineer explained: "A lot of the lab people don't like dealing with customers because they came to this company to do circuit design, or to design mechanical parts, not to deal on the phone with customers. If you try and make the R&D guys deal with customers, force them, you'll lose some of the technical experts. That can be dangerous."

Finally, to some engineers the focus on customers conveyed the message that technology was no longer valued, which meant that R&D engineers would no longer hold the high-status position they had for years. One engineer said that he had already seen evidence of this change: "R&D engineers have always been king of the hill in Test and Measurement. We were well rewarded and used to be held in high esteem. We used to have a lot of say in what goes on, and it was a nice environment to be in. That is changing. The need for good R&D people and the respect for them and trying to treat them well and trying to make the environment best for them is going away. That's this MBA attitude. We can just picture these people in corporate saying, 'Let's see, these engineers in R&D, what do they do? Do we need them?' People in finance probably figure 'Hell, we can just open the yellow pages and hire this engineering out.'"

To help overcome engineers' resistance, Thirumale visited the team frequently to explain how the changes in the division's external environment translated into the need for engineers to take on more responsibility and to become customer-focused. For example, at one of the initial meetings, Thirumale told a story of how, through a consultant, he had heard HP described as "slow, arrogant, conservative, bureaucratic, and inflexible." He continued: "That shows our history and baggage! We don't want to be that way any more. It represents the challenge we all face. The biggest obstacle is our T&M culture. It's not the HP culture. Other parts of HP— the laser printer business, for example—are fast, efficient, aggressive, and low-priced. So it's not necessarily tied to a company thing. There is no excuse for Santa Clara to be bureaucratic. We're not a Goliath."

Thirumale also used the "telephone game" (a game in which players standing in sequence attempt to keep a complex message intact as it passes down the line, whispered from ear to ear) as a metaphor to convey the need for engineers to talk directly to customers. "We need to get marketing out from between R&D and the customers," he said. "We've been playing the telephone game. Information comes back distorted. R&D engineers need to hear customers' needs directly, not through a whispering game." He used another example to convey the need for engineers to have business expertise in addition to technical expertise: "Ken [an R&D engineer] is on the plane right now on the way to visit a customer. If they ask him a question and he goes, 'Be de, be de, be de [Thirumale vibrates his lip with his finger], I need to call my boss,' we'll be just as slow as we were before. Ken should be the spokesperson for HP. Sure there's a risk that he'll say the wrong thing, but the alternative—centralizing all knowledge at the top of the organization—won't work. Engineers need to be able to speak about what we *will* do, not what we *might* do. That means they need more than technical information—they need *business understanding*. To make the sale Ken needs to understand that our strength in the clock business is strong distribution channels internationally—that's understanding that typically lab engineers don't have."

Finally, Thirumale used the visits to address controversial issues. In the following exchange, Thirumale addressed one R&D engineer's concern that becoming customer-driven would sacrifice the division's technological expertise by explaining that in the new organization, engineers—not managers—would be the ones to bid on projects and negotiate schedules:

R&D engineer: So you're saying, if the customer says he won't buy it unless we can make it in three months, but we know it will take nine months, you'll still tell us it has to be done in three months?

Thirumale: No! I won't be part of the picture. *You* will decide on what to bid!

R&D engineer: (so upset that he did not hear Thirumale's answer) We can't be only externally driven. We can't invent when the customer wants it. You make me nervous.

Thirumale: I'm talking about an interaction between the two. We need to find a way to operate in this environment where the impact of losing the bid is more significant than a cost overrun. We will have to get engineers much closer to customers because oftentimes deadlines are negotiable—and it will be your job to negotiate.

Through repeated discussions with Thirumale, the transition team members gradually began to understand the reasoning behind the redesign—and that the redesign was not, as many feared, "just another re-org." One engineer on the transition team said, "We're getting the picture. . . . We need to do something to enable the managers to focus on finding new customers and business opportunities. Without taking some responsibility away from them for running the business, so they don't have to worry about it so much, we won't survive. So I think a lot of us are beginning to see a need for the redesign." Other engineers on the transition team became convinced by the dramatic change in the division's structure. One said: "I see this redesign as quite different. In the past, we tended to take things apart and have people report to different structures, but the structures always remained the same. They'd just move product lines or people back and forth. But this appears to be a much more dramatic shift. The entire structure has changed, and teams are being given more responsibility than ever before."

Managers and engineers on the transition team attributed much of the uniqueness of the reorganization to Neil and his apparent commitment to bringing about fundamental change at the division. Engineers explained that they were first impressed with Neil's willingness to acknowledge that test and measurement was no longer a growing business. One engineer said: "Marty was the first division manager to come in and come up with a different answer. When he came in, he said, 'Test is dead. People aren't going to pay you a bunch of money for something they use for ten minutes and then put on a shelf for a year.' That was great."

Engineers were also impressed by Neil's apparent willingness to take risks and model the behavior he advocated. One engineer likened Neil to a good general and explained how he had taken a risk in letting selection committees hire the new CSMs: "Marty has been willing to take the kinds of risks that good generals do. Good generals leave themselves open to enough risks so you say, 'Wow. He's leaving himself open to possible failure,' yet at the same time they guide it along enough so it's not a failure. One of the things Marty did was get together selection committees to hire their bosses. That was the kind of risk that Marty was willing to take."

Finally, engineers were impressed by Neil's consistency and commitment to the redesign effort. One project manager said: "I think this reorganization is different from previous ones because in talking to Marty, he sounds really committed to making it work. He doesn't leap from good idea to good idea, jump around a lot. He has a pretty good idea of what he needs to do. So I feel like there's going to be some consistency and focus once changes are made. If we feel the changes are good, I think we'll stick with it for a while. I never saw anything this dramatic. Marty has a pretty good insight of what the problems are, of what's going on. I think he'll work on it hard enough until it gets fixed. He won't just go away."

Once the engineers on the transition team had a better understanding of how and why the division had to change, they were able to turn their attention to the task at hand: aligning the division's structure and culture with its new values. Never having redesigned an organization before, however, most engineers on the transition team were at a loss as to where to start. They had heard about terms such as "matrix structure" and "team-based incentive systems" but had little idea what they really meant. To help the transition team learn about organizational design—especially those in nonlinear, or knowledge-work environments—Brandenmuehl arranged for the team to conduct benchmarking visits to HP's Eastern Sales Support office in Parkridge, New Jersey, and to Champion Paper in Nyack, New York, where the transition team learned about work redesign in nonmanufacturing environments. The team found Champion Paper, which began a work redesign effort in its corporate technology group in 1989, particularly instructive because it was the first successful work redesign the division knew of in a highly technical environment. The team returned from the benchmarking visits with firsthand knowledge about organizational design and were convinced that the best scheme for the division's internal structure would be a modified matrix structure.

For their technical analysis the transition team reviewed the NPD team's findings about the problems in the new product development process. Two engineers served on both the NPD team and the transition team;

thus they shared with the transition team the findings from both the 6X postpartum and the NPD's analysis of the new product development process.

As engineers on the transition team worked through the Bull's-Eye, first reviewing the findings from the business analysis, the technical analysis, and then the analysis of the division's internal structure, they began to question the lengthiness of the approach in light of the division's urgent situation. One engineer on the transition team explained: "We're going through a very long, planned process to gather a lot of data, analyze it, and make decisions. As an engineer, I can certainly understand the importance of doing that. But in this case I question, are we really gathering data that's going to help us make these decisions, or do we already know what we need to do, and the data is just something we're just gathering to see if it supports our views? I have a strong feeling that that's what's happening. In the R&D lab, there's not a lot of negativity about the fact that we needed to go through the reorganization itself, but there was some feeling that the Bull's-Eye, the interviewing, and some of the techniques that we were using was going overboard in terms of the method—a lot of show, but maybe not a lot of substance. So I have some reservations about the process, more than about the results."

Several engineers on the transition team explained that the STS approach did not appeal to their peers because engineers, in general, had little affinity for the "social" aspects. One manager on the transition team joked that if the term read "technosocial system" it would stand a better change of being accepted. The Bull's-Eye, in particular, became a source of resistance. One transition team member said, "The Bull's-Eye is interesting but esoteric. It's something we'd study in school, but how do we apply it to the division?" The Bull's-Eye also became the butt of many jokes. Some engineers joked that it would make a good dart board. One engineer said: "In talking to my friends here, I'd get, 'Oh, you're on the *Bull's-Eye* team.' The Bull's-Eye is not a popular concept in the R&D lab. It's viewed as a gimmick, a lot of window dressing. It's unfair to say that it's a negative thing, but it's a source of many humorous comments. For example, engineers will joke, 'Oh, I'm having problems designing this printed circuit board. Maybe I should just draw a Bull's-Eye on a piece of paper and it will tell me how I should do my design.'"

Over time, however, the engineers on the team began to see some value in the STS model. One explained, "The Bull's-Eye still has a strong negative connotation in peoples' minds as a management fad. Unless you understand it, it turns you off. Now that I've used it, I think it's a terrific tool."

Seven months into their eight-month time frame, the transition team still had not conducted the social analysis or investigated the division's systems of evaluation, pay, and training. Several fretted about not having enough time to do a good job. One manager on the team said, "There's just not enough time. I'd need twenty more hours per week to feel good about the work I'm contributing to this effort." Another said, "We'd like to be able to put in more hours on this team, but we all have full-time jobs and families at home. I for one have a wife and kids, and don't want to work from 7 A.M. to 7 P.M." One engineer explained that even his boss was starting to worry that being on the transition team was taking too much time away from his regular job. Ultimately, the team decided that some part of the STS analysis would have to go. One member of the team summed up the dilemma: "The initial strategy was to educate us, then do the proposal. I'm not educated enough, but we have to move on."

As a result, the team decided to focus primarily on the organization's structure and leave investigations into the division's support systems (e.g., evaluations, rewards, and training) for a later date. They would outsource the social analysis to our UCLA research team and learn from its findings. The social analysis would attempt to measure the alignment of the division's culture with its new values and would include two components: a written survey that would be administered to the entire division and focus groups with managers and engineers to investigate their reactions to the new values in greater depth.

The social analysis revealed that most of the values at the heart of the HP Way were still strong. The majority of engineers felt that they were treated with trust and respect and that they could count on others for help when they needed it. They still took great pride in their work and were glad to work for the division. The survey also revealed, however, the complexity of adopting several of the new values:

Customer focus: The majority of engineers agreed that the division needed to get better at scanning the environment for business opportunities and acknowledged that they too would have to focus more on customers' needs. Over two-thirds, however, still feared that the new customer focus was a threat to the division's commitment to technology.

Accountability: Virtually all managers and engineers agreed on the importance of meeting commitments to reduce the cost of bringing new products to market. They explained, however, that they were often pressured into giving management unrealistic schedules so as to get projects approved and that historically there were no consequences for failing to meet deadlines. They also pointed out that they should not be punished for failing to meet commitments when delays were outside their control.

Empowerment: Most managers said they wanted engineers to take on more responsibility but recognized that they were "spread so thin" that this would be difficult. They also pointed out that engineers needed more training in business aspects such as how to compute ROI or how to make financial justifications. Some engineers, in turn, said they wanted to have more "say" in which projects the division chose to pursue, but there was no clear process for doing so. Moreover, they pointed out that their ideas were sometimes "shot down" because managers did not think they would lead to immediate profits.

Flexibility and teamwork: Managers and engineers pointed out that "working as a team," which they defined as working in informal project teams, was historically part of HP's culture. They differentiated between "working as a team," and "teamwork" however, and explained that they distrusted management's use of the latter term because they interpreted it as a ploy to coerce them to volunteer for jobs they did not want. Engineers said they were willing to accept changes in their work assignments to help the division survive, but voiced a clear preference for staying in R&D.

The transition team discussed the findings from the social analysis during one of their weekly meetings. There were few surprises, members agreed, because they had come across many of the same themes in discussions with their peers and in reviewing the findings from the NPD team. The main outcome of the social analysis was the team's decision to create incentives for engineers to motivate them to take on more responsibility for projects' results.

In late July, the transition team members met for a two-day-long meeting at a Catholic retreat hidden in a residential Sunnyvale neighborhood to pull together their findings and develop their proposal for a new internal organizational design. As a first step, before working as a group, the engineers on the transition team presented their "personal proposals," or their ideas of how they would redesign the internal organization if it were solely up to them. Having engineers brainstorm initially on their own or in small groups, explained Brandemuehl, would help exhaust the range of possible new organizational designs. After engineers discovered that their personal proposals had several common themes, they agreed on three that would form the basis of the new TSC organization: a matrix structure, a "free market" concept, and team empowerment.[4]

Incorporating Neil's suggestion, the team based the matrix structure on the program leader concept and proposed the creation of four program leaders to lead TSC's businesses. As explained by the transition team members, the matrix structure would enable the program leaders and customer

4. These changes would apply only to the new TSC organization because the manager of the laser business chose to be excluded from the redesign. He believed, and Naylor agreed, that the laser business was already operating effectively.

segment managers to focus on the "strategic" aspects of the business by freeing them from the "tactical" or administrative tasks, which, in turn, would be taken care of by the support organizations (NPPS and Order Fulfillment). As "owners" of their specific business segments, the program leaders would control the program budget, negotiate resources, and initiate or lead teams as needed. They would be evaluated based on their contributions to the profit or loss of that business segment. They would have no direct reports, thus freeing them up to become externally focused, flexible, and responsive to customers' demands. Finally, they would actively contribute to engineers' evaluations but would not be responsible for them.

The decision as to whether there should be project leaders would be left up to engineers. Project leaders could be recruited by program leaders or the CSMs to spearhead projects. Project leaders would have a temporary role rather than a permanent position in the organization. In other words, an individual could be a project leader on one project and a team member on the next.

The transition team decided that the matrix structure should operate as a "free market" to provide engineers with more "voice and choice" in picking projects. Engineers would be free to choose the projects on which they wished to work, rather than be assigned, or could be recruited directly by a program leader. Program leaders would interpret engineers' choices as a vote that the technology or product was worthwhile for the division to pursue. To ensure that engineers chose projects based on their merit alone, rather than their project managers' "position power," engineers would *not* report to program leaders. Like lawyers in a law firm, engineers would be responsible for their own time management and setting priorities and would bill out the majority of their time to clients (program and project leaders). They would have to satisfy their customers to be in demand. In turn, program leaders would have to be viewed as "respected leaders" to attract engineers to work on their programs.

The free market, the design team members reasoned, would be self-regulated by "checks and balances." In other words, if a program leader were ineffective, he or she would be unable to recruit engineers. Similarly, if an engineer were ineffective, he or she would have trouble obtaining a position on a project. The team agreed on a set of ground rules to ensure that the free market concept ran fairly. Communication would have to be open, and there would be no "under the table" deals. In other words, program leaders could selectively recruit engineers but would have to do so openly with the knowledge of all other engineers. Anyone could submit ideas for projects by using forms designed for that purpose, and all project ideas would be evaluated on merit using a common set of measures.

Finally, the new TSC organization would be built on seven different types of teams. First, a team made up of Neil's staff would conduct strategic planning, authorize funds to start building products, and approve incentives designed to reward project teams for meeting deadlines. Program teams would manage each business's strategy and growth. Cross-functional new product development teams would conceive and design new products. Cross-functional SDBS teams would customize existing products for new customers. Cross-functional ad hoc/special project teams, such as the transition team, would investigate issues and provide recommendations as needed. Function (e.g., R&D or marketing) teams would help engineers learn new skills (e.g., how to calculate ROI), find tools, and share best practices. Sales and service teams would help engineers market and support existing products.[5]

During the off-site meeting, several emotional issues emerged. One was what to do about the predicted 15 percent of the population who would be unable to make the changes being suggested. One engineer provided an example: "I know an engineer who would be really uncomfortable being responsible for sales because he's never sold anything in his life. He refuses to call up customers. What will happen to people like him who can't adapt?" "They'll be at a disadvantage," said one engineer. The financial analyst responded, "But we can't ignore the nonadapters, and we'll have to deal with them, otherwise they'll pull the new structure down." Taking a different stance, one manager suggested, "Maybe they should simply look for jobs elsewhere." Taken aback at this suggestion, an R&D engineer responded: "We're increasing peoples' freedom to control their destiny, but are we also holding them accountable if they don't? We're HP, not Apple. I view HP as a family. You don't cut family members off because they're not doing something well." Although the team members remained divided on this issue, they agreed on the need to provide a variety of training and educational opportunities to accommodate employees' different learning styles and help them adapt to the changes they were being asked to make.

A second issue that surfaced was engineers' resistance to being evaluated as a team. An engineer explained: "How can you hold a manufacturing engineer responsible when an R&D engineer can't get an IC [integrated circuit] to work? How will marketing and manufacturing feel if the R&D process is too slow? Or an R&D engineer if the graphic designers are too slow? How will people feel when their performance is pulling down the entire team's evaluation?" Several members on the team ex-

---

5. The transition team defined the purpose, responsibilities, decisions owned, knowledge, information and skills required, staffing, and incentives for each type of team. This information was too detailed to include here; thus this discussion is limited to each team's purpose.

plained: "That's where the free market would kick in. The team would decide on whether or not poor performers would stay or go."

Several days after the meeting, in early August, the transition team presented its proposal to the steering committee. The steering committee accepted the proposal, believing that it was consistent with the division's new values.

REACTIONS TO THE PROPOSAL

The next step was for the transition team to present its proposal to the workforce. This was accomplished through several hour-long coffee talks held at various times and locations throughout the division. After one coffee talk, employees were invited to attend small group sessions hosted by a pair of transition team members, with no managers present, to air their reactions to the proposal over a free lunch. Throughout the communication sessions, the transition team members stressed that their proposal was just a recommendation and that "nothing was cast in concrete."

The luncheon feedback sessions revealed that employees' initial reactions to the proposal were lukewarm at best. Most engineers voiced the same concerns as had transition team members originally. The two most common concerns were that the reorganization was the wrong solution to the division's business situation and that the customer focus would threaten the division's commitment to technology. Engineers' resistance to the proposal became clear when, during one feedback session, several demanded that a vote be taken. "There must be an avenue for people to express whether or not to go ahead with this," one exclaimed. The transition team member obliged, saying, "I'd be crazy to say no." The group voted on a scale of 0 (complete disagreement) to 5 (complete agreement). The average score was 2.8.

The feedback sessions also revealed, however, the benefit of having team members themselves—rather than managers—design, present, and advocate the new design. During one session, engineers voiced their skepticism freely, inundating the transition team member with questions and criticisms that many engineers later said would not have surfaced if a manager were present. Because the transition team member was also an engineer, his responses appeared to carry more weight with his peers than if they had come from a manager. For example, when several engineers voiced their concern that the new customer focus would sacrifice the division's technological leadership, the transition team member responded: "What distinguishes us is our technology. We can't let that change, and we won't. But if a customer wants us to build a product just for them, we'll have to listen. Unless we build products that customers want, we won't be around much longer to build *anything*!" One of the engineers who had raised the concern responded, "I never thought I'd hear that from you. I guess it *must* be true."

In another example, engineers worried that "MBA-minded managers" would approve only "grand slams," rather than "base hits." To this concern the transition team member responded, "No! In the new structure, *we* will run projects. Engineers can go off and form a team around any technology they want. But we'll also have to recognize when a new technology is a dead end! The definition of a team's success will be when it can start or cancel a project by itself." Sitting back in his chair as the idea gradually sank in, the concerned engineer said, "Wow. That will be a real cultural change. We used to say, 'I hope *they* won't cancel a project. Now *we* are *they*!'"

Several weeks later the design team assembled one last time for lunch at an Italian restaurant several blocks from the plant to recognize their accomplishment. Brandemuehl gave each member a unique gift as well as a miniature "Etch-A-Sketch" (a children's drawing toy) humorously to acknowledge their new expertise at being organizational designers.

After the transition team's last meeting, the team members came together to conduct their own postpartum, which was also attended by Neil. The most pressing issue that arose during this meeting was the enormous amount of time that engineers had spent on developing the proposal. After commending the transition team members for their efforts and final proposal, which one engineer proudly equated to a "master's thesis on organizational design," Neil asked how many person-hours the entire project had taken. The team calculated twelve hundred (based on an average of ten hours per person per week for twelve weeks). This was more than double the amount of time planned. Neil exclaimed, "Twelve hundred person-hours! We can't spend this much doing these transitions if we are going to redo the division. Ranking is in the 1994 Hoshin. That will be a thousand-person-hour job also. I know you all have full-time jobs, but I'm asking you to do it even faster. We can't take that long next time." Momentarily taken aback, the transition team members explained that now that they understood how to gather the necessary data, analyze organizations as systems, and work together, they could accomplish subsequent redesigns in a far shorter time. They assured Neil, "It won't take us that long again because we know how to do it now."

IMPLEMENTING THE NEW ORGANIZATIONAL DESIGN

The structural components of the new TSC organization were implemented over the course of several months beginning in mid-August 1993.

The transition team meetings ended, and most engineers on the team returned to working full-time on their jobs. Several senior engineers from the team continued meeting informally to help implement the free market concept. A free market bulletin board displaying all existing and available projects was posted in the aisle in the R&D section. Teams made up of managers, engineers, and other employees formed to interview candidates for the new program leader positions and hired program leaders to run the four new business programs.

In October 1993, a team of seven engineers from R&D and marketing was recruited to pilot the new SDBS strategy. The team would be self-managing, explained Brandemuehl, and the first engineering team to work without a project manager. The team would be responsible for bringing in millions of dollars over the course of one year by writing software to customize the division's general-purpose modulation domain analyzers (or MDAs) according to customers' needs. (The MDA is an instrument that isolates and characterizes the underlying causes of unwanted signal variation, called "jitter," from electronic products such as disk drives, CD players, and telecommunications equipment.) The team would then sell the software packages to customers such as IBM, Seagate, and Northern Telecom.

The SDBS team was expected to have only a limited financial impact on the division. Its real significance was as a test case of two of the division's new organizational principles: self-managing teams of engineers and the SDBS strategy. According to Brandemuehl, the team of engineers was given a "bucket of money," full responsibility for the business, control of the budget, and then left alone. Team members would be responsible for finding their own customers and deciding among themselves which products to build and which deals to pursue.

Initial changes were also made to the division's performance evaluation and pay systems. Teams would now be held accountable for meeting project deadlines, and failure to do so would be reflected in employees' performance evaluations. "The major change will be that teams are evaluated based on results, not activity," Brandemuehl explained. She added, however, that factors such as whether a project was "high risk" or if steps required to meet the deadline were out of the teams' control would be taken into account in evaluating a team's performance.[6]

6. In 1995, the division was experimenting with applying HP's ranking system to entire teams. This meant that if a team met its deadline, everyone on the team would get the same ranking. Employees' overall individual rankings would then be based on the percentage of their time spent on each project.

EARLY IMPROVEMENTS IN THE NEW PRODUCT DEVELOPMENT PROCESS

While the new TSC organizational design was being implemented, the new product development process was reengineered. In a dramatic departure from the past, the PC Layout Department was shut down, and the process was outsourced to a vendor who could do the work more competitively. The product specification phase of the new product development process was standardized, which led to immediate improvements. According to Mark Allen, the first product that was developed after the reengineering "went through like butter. All the product definition work had been done up front and was communicated before the lab started working on it. The project was on time and on budget."

Further to reduce product slippages, project teams would conduct midcourse reviews every quarter, regardless of the stage of the project, rather than after it was completed. This, Allen explained, would help the teams meet their deadlines by giving them the opportunity to take stock of their progress, reevaluate the schedule, and adjust it if necessary. In addition, third-party facilitators would conduct postpartums on every project to find ways projects could be better managed.

EASING ANXIETY

Neil knew that the redesign and the division's dire business situation were exacting a toll on employees' morale. To lift their spirits and help them cope with the changes, one evening Neil treated the entire division to a dinner followed by a skit in Santa Clara's comfortable cafeteria. HP skits, a ritual that dates back to the company's early days, are typically intended for fun but also serve to reaffirm HP's strong culture in times of stress. This one was designed to bring out the heavy issues that Neil knew were on the minds of the division's employees—declining revenue, job security, worries about the new business, and engineers' reluctance to become customer-focused. The skit, however, was kept a secret until the last minute. Throughout the day, employees were told only that there would be a fantastic dinner speaker, one they would be "sorry to miss."

That evening after dinner, Neil took the podium to introduce the guest speaker. Instead, a man dressed like a 1960s hippie appeared on the stage. Strumming a guitar and playing a harmonica to the tune of the Bob Dylan favorite "The Times They Are A'Changin," he sang lyrics that had been tailored for Santa Clara:

Come gather round, Santa Clara,
Wherever you roam,
And admit the changes around you have grown . . .
Now that every damn budget's been cut to the bone,
Here's something you'll find agitatin'—
Only the ants are the ones with a home!

Oh, the times they are a'changin'!

Once we had Sandblaster [a reference to a failed project],
Oh, boy was it chic.
Then it went south, and we were up shit creek,
Now we've got a new business, that's *really* unique,
Since they came up with S Y N C H R O N I Z A T I O N,
And if we're really lucky, it might last a week!

Oh, the times they are a'changin'!

Now the times, they sure are tough at HP,
It's a good thing that Corporate is there to help me!
And transition teams—they are their strategy,
And surely they'll be our salvation!
But the Bull's-Eye ain't the only bull that I see!

Oh, the times they are a'changin'!

By the middle of the song, employees had recovered from their shock, realized the skit was a spoof, and were laughing hysterically, clapping and singing. After several more skits and roasts, the evening ended with a ballad sung by an engineer dressed up like the stereotypical nerd—exaggerated buck teeth, clothed in plaid pants and sneakers, with calculators and rulers falling out of his pockets. Dancing awkwardly to the loud music, he sang:

I was born, in on-line mode,
When it comes to brains, I've got a truck load,
I was educated, at MIT
And graduated, with a Double E!

I'm a lab man, R&D man,
I'm a lab man, R&D man.

Promise plenty, deliver less,
What you'll get, is anybody's guess.
If my name shows up on the list,
I'll hide in my cube and try to be missed!
Dress me up, take me out, and then
I'll see customers, but
just don't make me talk to them!

I'm a lab man, R&D man,
I'm a lab man, hardware man!

By the end of the program, employees were wiping tears of laughter from their eyes. While the event had raised issues and emotions that were painfully true, confronting them together reaffirmed the HP "family feeling" so often described by employees. Most knew that the transition to a new organization had just begun, but as one employee commented, "at least we know we're in it together."

1994: A YEAR OF TRANSITION

Despite attempts to keep up morale, the year following the implementation of the new organizational design was a difficult one for the Santa Clara Division. A tremendous amount of progress had been made; the division had been restructured, and after an intensive search a new business direction had been identified. Yet by March of 1994, almost two years after the redesign began, there had been little change in the division's bottom line. In fact, the division was facing what Thirumale called the "revenue chasm of 1994." In the existing business, five new products were near their release dates and approximately a dozen others were being developed. Orders, however, remained few and far between. As a result, the projected 1994 revenue had been scaled back.

The biggest concern was that the new business, Sync, would not "ramp up" fast enough to survive. During one meeting held to review the division's progress, CSM Thirumale explained: "There is a tangible business in Sync. We have lots of product ideas and products, but the world is not aware. We have more Sync marketing to do—road shows, customer visits, etc. We are behind. We're missing the market. We need to get the funnel filled up to get confidence and revenue ramped up fast. There's a big gap. My concern is that the current businesses are eroding faster than we can ramp up Sync, and time will run out."

In the absence of new business, most employees held a "wait and see" attitude about the value of the redesign. "The jury's still out," many said.

"We're hanging in limbo," explained an R&D engineer. "We're still in a downward trend, and the actions that have been taken as part of the restructuring haven't had a chance to take effect yet." Another described the chaos of being in transition: "We're in the interim, hanging by a thread. We've destroyed the old system. All the communications that made the old system work are severed. Everyone's running around, doing different things, but we're not sure what we're doing." Another said, "There's a lull in morale. We're waiting to see how the new system works, but we don't know yet because everyone is learning their new job. Things haven't jelled, so it's of no value yet. We're all going to school on the new system." Others were less sanguine: "I'll believe it when I see it. There have been too many holy grails."

The restructuring, combined with years of gradual downsizing and Neil's efforts to communicate, had an effect on employees' sense of urgency. The manager of the model shop explained, "The division has been very antsy for quite a while since we've gone through a number of annual downsizings. Everyone's pretty aware if we're not successful at what we're doing, bad things are going to happen." Neil diligently kept employees abreast of the division's dire business situation. "Marty sends out daily sales figures," one engineer explained, "so we know that orders are way down. I look at the daily sales reports and realize that's what's paying my salary. We know that next month, we could be out of business. Job security is an illusion. Marty wants us to hear the bad news as fast as he does so that if he has to lay people off, he'll know he gave you as much warning as he could have." Another engineer said, "This reorg is like getting a D on your report card. You got a bad grade, and you know why. We're at that cusp. We know we're in trouble."

With fewer people, some engineers were forced to become more flexible simply because they had to take on a wider variety of tasks to get them done. A marketing engineer explained: "We're down to the bare bones. Everybody's juggling more and more balls, trying not to drop them." Similarly, an R&D engineer said: "As the teams get smaller, you have to take on more and more jobs, otherwise we couldn't survive. In the old days, you'd have twelve R&D engineers and a couple of marketing and manufacturing engineers on a team, and R&D engineers would stick to doing R&D. Now everyone's equal. I do marketing and manufacturing stuff, where reasonable."

An estimated 10 to 20 percent of engineers, however, remained unwilling to work across functions. Some of them decided to leave the division. One engineer explained: "It's bogus that they take a person from one function and want them to do another. They wanted this one R&D engineer to go to marketing. They tried to twist his arm and he left the division—went back to HP Labs [a corporate facility that engages in advanced research to help lead the company into new technologies]. R&D or marketing people never lose their identity. People don't just switch over. If you try to make them, they'll leave."

Greater awareness of the need to meet commitments—and the consequences of not meeting them—gradually began to filter down through the ranks as a result of Neil and Thirumale's frequent communication and encouragement. For instance, when engineers came to Thirumale with a new idea, he would say, "What a great idea! I can see it's exciting. But tell me: What kind of ROI will it bring in?" Thirumale knew that such a challenge would motivate engineers to take a finance class or to talk with the business analyst about how to calculate ROI.

Changing performance evaluations so that engineers were now measured on the basis of results, rather than activity, also had a significant effect on their behavior. One engineer explained: "Marty has sent out a memo on accountability—it's Monday Memo #27. It talks about how we're consistently not meeting our results in less discretionary spending, meeting deadlines, and trying new ideas, which will ultimately result in lower ranking and a different job. Some people dismiss it. I don't." One manager explained: "I see a definite recognition that accountability, and being measured on results versus commitment, is getting through to people. The managers preparing evaluations are documenting both expected and actual project times, which factors into engineers' performance evaluations. That makes engineers take deadlines seriously."

The free market, a popular concept with engineers, began showing signs of success in the few programs that were developing new products. A project leader explained: "Engineers now have more input into our top-level product decisions. We rely more heavily on who wants to work on projects and are giving engineers more weight in terms of what they think we should be working on. We take their vote as an indication that the project is worthwhile. Before, decisions about which products to develop were made at the functional staff level, and engineers' input was limited. Now we throw four or five projects out and see which engineers sign up for them and take them as a vote for the projects."

For most engineers, however, in the absence of new projects, the free market concept remained largely untested. One engineer explained: "The 'free' part is very encouraging. But the 'market' part—the field in which we're going to play—is unknown right now. The business strategy needs to be in place first. Then folks can see the free market as an opportunity, and the pieces of the puzzle will be there. But now the free market is unknown, and the business direction is unknown, so it's almost crippling.

People say, 'I'll wait. When they get the strategy figured out I'll figure out how to play.'"

Perhaps the most difficult new behavior for engineers to develop was focusing on customers. One explained: "Marty would like it for engineers to go on customer visits and talk to customers one-on-one to find out exactly what they're doing—what their application is and what they need—because engineers, with their technical expertise, would have a better understanding of what the customer is having trouble with than a high-level manager who is not up to speed technically." The problem, as managers and engineers explained, was that many engineers found the experience of working with customers either undesirable, unenjoyable, or uncomfortable. "My experience with most electrical engineers," said one manager, "is that they have a hard time dealing with other people because they don't have a lot of interpersonal skills. Some do—some have the kind of personality that will allow them to be conversational etc., and they have the technical skills as well. But I think engineers who have all those skills are a rare breed." Another manager put it this way: "HP is an introverted company. We believe that the best ideas come from within. By trying to become more customer-focused, we're trying to become an extrovert. Do you know how hard it is to change an introvert to an extrovert?"

In many cases, engineers explained that they understood the need to work with customers, but when it came down to actually calling them on the telephone or going out to visit them, they procrastinated. One engineer explained: "Knowing intellectually that we had to talk to customers and internalizing it—actually doing it—is a different matter. I subscribe to the need to talk to customers, but only on the intellectual level, not on the emotional level. I give myself excuses like, I 'gotta debut this software,' or we 'gotta get this product out.' While these are valid reasons, I know they are not enough to stop me from calling up customers for twenty minutes each day. A guy like me needs a kick in the right places."

The most obvious way for engineers to begin working with customers was to mimic what project managers and marketing engineers did regularly—call them up and arrange a visit. Doing so, however, was not so easy. A program leader explained: "In the ideal world, engineers would be able to call up customers and initiate visits themselves. But without some prior experience in meeting customers for the first time, this is unrealistic." He continued: "It's like going to a foreign country. If you've never done it before, you don't know the protocol, the customs. The willingness and interest are there, but many engineers are not comfortable with business etiquette and the culture of selling. They ask questions like, 'What do I say? What do I do? I don't know how to talk to people.' They don't know what they should or shouldn't say in front of a customer, or how to dress."

The next best approach was for engineers to accompany project managers on customer visits, a practice that occurred relatively frequently and with significant success. One project manager explained: "I've taken a bunch of guys out with me . . . they tell me it helps because they don't feel like they're under the spotlight, yet at the same time they can observe how we interact. Engineers are conscientious people—after a while they loosen up—and, even if they don't realize it, they always contribute with their technical knowledge. They often follow up on a customer's comment and ask technical, clarifying questions that a marketing person wouldn't know to ask."

When project managers could not bring engineers to customers, they tried to bring the customers to them. Bringing customers into the division's R&D section, however, could be risky. One manager explained: "Leaving engineers alone with customers inside the division can be dangerous. Often engineers don't know the standards of business conduct, and they tend to treat customers the same way they treat each other. We've had several embarrassing situations happen already. One time, an engineer walked a customer right down the aisle where all our sales history and proprietary information was displayed!"

Despite these mistakes, bringing customers to the division worked well and even produced unanticipated benefits. An R&D engineer explained: "In the Wildlife project, we brought the customer to the division to work directly with the cesium team. It worked pretty well. The engineers got involved with the customer and talked on a fairly regular basis. What ended up happening was that the product developed as the customer's desires evolved! The box we were originally going to build for the customer is not the box we will build now. It has features the customer didn't ask for in the beginning. So the team and the customer locked in at the right time, just as the customer's vision was jelling."

TESTING THE NEW ORGANIZATIONAL PRINCIPLES

As 1994 came to a close, evidence that the division's new principles were taking root began to appear. This was most evident in two teams— the SDBS team that had formed in late 1993 to pilot the new SDBS strategy and an ad hoc team of engineers that came together on a moment's notice to pursue the division's first potential Sync deal.

In October 1993, the SDBS team came to life. At first glance, the most obvious difference between it and other teams the division was the absence of a project leader—a first for R&D in the division. Typically, an engineer on the team explained, the R&D project leader oversees the logistics of developing a new product, such as making sure it was completed on schedule and getting it onto the corporate price list, leaving the engineers to focus on creating. "The project leader," the engineer explained, "was the objective leader who would say no to 'creeping featurism'—our tendency to keep adding features to the product just because we think they're neat—and say 'just ship the damn thing!'"

Suddenly responsible for everything from inventing the software to making sure the finished products were shipped on time, engineers on the SDBS team felt swamped. The complexity of their task was reflected in their daily half-hour meetings. The team's engineers, who previously had been solely concerned with inventing technology, now discussed whose turn it was to find the next customer, who would write the start-up guide, how they would price the product, when it should be posted on the corporate price list, when it would be shipped, and how they would train the field engineers to market and sell it. Overwhelmed and overloaded, engineers worried that these critical steps would "fall through the cracks."

Determined to prove their autonomy, the engineers on the SDBS team soon devised mechanisms to substitute for a project manager. For instance, to make sure nothing fell through the cracks, they developed a checklist to make sure they took care of all the necessary logistics. They also established relationships with people in the surrounding support departments such as graphics, manufacturing, and sales, who would help them package and ship the products when the time came.

Despite initial difficulties, the engineers soon came to prefer working without a project manager. Several said they liked the feeling of sharing risk and accountability. "We like not having a manager because now we all share responsibility. The competition between us is also more healthy than when you have a boss. Everyone carries their own weight and we judge each other as peers. You want to appear efficient in the eyes of your peers. There is no nebulous person, no boss, who is supposed to know all. If I don't know something, then others probably don't either. It's shared. We are all concerned. Now we all bite our nails together!" By sharing risk, another explained, the team could take on even more: "When one person takes the risk, he can end up in the mud. But on the SDBS team, there is more risk-taking because the consequences are diluted. We rely on others and can tolerate more ambiguity because we're united."

The Emergence of New Behaviors

As the engineers on the SDBS team learned how to work as a self-managing team, many of the desired new behaviors outlined by the division's new values began to emerge. For example, R&D and marketing engineers became more aware of each others' responsibilities and more willing to help each other out. One marketing engineer explained: "R&D is getting a better idea of the marketing limitations I face, and I am learning what's involved in software development." An R&D engineer on the team was overjoyed when a marketing engineer learned and appreciated the complexity entailed in his R&D work. He explained: "Several days ago, one of our marketing people came to my cubicle to suggest a software change and convinced me that it really needed to be done. Thinking it would only take a second, he sat and waited while I went to my computer and made a few changes. He said, 'Oh, that was easy.' I said, 'Wait a minute, it's not done yet.' I had to change this file, and this file, and this file. He'd never seen that done before and asked, 'How do you know you have to make all those changes? How do you know you don't miss one?' I explained that you don't always know—that's the tricky part—and that a minor change can have lots of implications. But the point is, I was delighted that the person who was asking for the change was suddenly sitting here, realizing that even though it appears to be a very simple change on the surface, there is a tremendous amount of underneath stuff that you have to worry about and check."

Working across functional boundaries made the process of developing new products far more efficient. One engineer explained: "In the past, John [an R&D engineer] would go off developing stuff he thought was whizzy even before he fully understood the usefulness of it. Sometimes he'd come up with a brilliant product but there was simply no application for it. Now Bill [a sales engineer] is steering him real time toward products that there's a market for. Of course there has to be a balance—John still needs to be able to invent on his own because he can think up things that the customer hasn't even thought of. The point is, this type of interaction never happened before. Before, Bill would have to talk with his product marketing manager who would then talk to John's R&D section manager, and *eventually* Bill and John might talk."

Now accountable for meeting their deadlines, engineers became more careful about how they were set. "In the past," one explained, "the project manager would have gone off and said, 'OK, we're going to shoot for February.' We'd agree, even if we knew we were not going to make it. But now, we all feel accountable. We know why it's important to ship in February, so we're more realistic in setting our goals. That increases the chances that if we say we'll ship in February, we really will. We may still not meet the deadline—but if we don't, it won't be because we agreed to unrealistic goals; it'll be because we really couldn't, and we'll have the right to reset it."

Sharing accountability across the entire team also reduced the tendency to blame each other, or "point fingers." One engineer explained what happened after a project missed its deadline: "Our goal was to ship at the end of December. As we went along, we realized that that wasn't going to happen, and it didn't. In the past, the marketing people would point fingers at the lab, or the lab people would blame marketing. Now that we are all involved in making the decision, we all understood why we couldn't ship by the end of December, and nobody got mad."

Facing customers was harder for the engineers on the SDBS team, but it was a skill that they would have to acquire to develop products that customers wanted to buy. Their program leader explained: "It's a learning that has to take place, because now we have to do it. Finding customers is a panning for gold sort of thing. The group does not have super high skills in prospecting, but that's not surprising since we haven't hired people for that. But they'll have to acquire the ability to prospect and scan the environment to meet their goal."

One engineer who bore the title of "senior scientist" (the highest professional rank an HP engineer can receive) explained his reluctance to talk to customers. "I like to know what I'm talking about before I really talk to someone," he said. "But in talking to a customer, it is very likely that he would be in an area in which I know very little. I would sound very ignorant, and sound very stupid and foolish, when I am simply uninformed about a subject." He continued: "The worst fear comes when a customer waits silently for you to ask them a question, and after you do they answer just yes or no, and then you have to think of something else to say."

The SDBS program leader explained how he helped engineers get past their fears. "I try to encourage them to relax and be themselves," he said. "We role-play customer visits before we go out and then analyze each role to demystify the process of selling. I try to get them to see that everyone's there for a purpose. The customer wants a certain product at a certain price, and we want to sell it. But engineers have never been used to thinking in those terms, so it requires a new perspective."

To help themselves gain this new perspective, engineers practiced their customer "spiels" with each other during their weekly meetings. One morning, for instance, after reviewing the meeting's agenda and figuring out how to debug a new product, the topic shifted back to customer visits. One engineer passed around a spiel several marketing engineers had written to advertise a new product. In high spirits, the team clamored for someone to read it aloud. After clearing his throat self-consciously, one engineer began reading like a door-to-door salesman making a pitch: "Hey *Pete* [a fictitious customer]! I have a new HP product for measuring *Token Ring jitter*. Sounds like it was made just for *you*. It does all the interoperability jitter tests you need. . . . It even captures continuous edges in a single shot. I don't know of any other product that can do *that*! And what's *really great*—it records billions of edges at the rate of the clock so you can get true peak-to-peak jitter in seconds. You can even see cycle-to-cycle jitter. Can we set a time to *talk* more about it?"

The only way for engineers truly to learn how to deal with customers, the SDBS program leader maintained, was to do so on the job where the consequences were real. "I'm from the school of hard knocks," he said. "I have engineers go out and visit customers, face to face, rather than over the telephone, because it yields volumes more learning. I do anything to encourage hands-on experience and to foster interaction with people. Role playing is great preparation but it's artificial, and you can't make it hurt. You have to sweat for it. There were expectations by upper management that this conversion would simply happen. We want all of our people to think of this team as their own small business and to run it that way. But it's a long-term change we're after, and it won't happen overnight."

After accompanying the program leader on customer visits, engineers gradually became more willing to visit customers on their own. One explained that visiting customers became much easier when he was provided with leads. He explained: "What really helps is when someone gives me a name—then I am much more tempted to follow up with this person. It's less scary and more purposeful. Or sometimes a potential customer will call with a technical question, and the person will pass the customer on to me. When I talk to a customer about an area in which I'm knowledgeable, then I am more tempted, more motivated to talk to customers. Then the hardest part is the first few minutes. Once I get started, particularly if I'm talking to the right person and we talk shop, suddenly the whole thing blossoms, and it becomes very exciting."

A Three Hundred Hour Response Time

Evidence that the new principles were being adopted also surfaced in a team that coalesced to build a custom timing product for the division's first potential Sync customer. The opportunity arose when a well-known telecommunications company called Qualcomm that specialized in wireless technology notified the division that it was looking for a supplier to design a prototype clock to install in a new wireless communication system. "They want a clock that will emit a one-second pulse that is rock steady and works for years," explained Thirumale, the CSM for Sync. "They also want it to be cheap!"

The division was asked to respond within sixteen days—a cycle time which, Thirumale said, was "unprecedented" for the division. "Yet," he explained, "this was the moment we were waiting for. This opportunity could open a door to the new communication information systems marketplace and could be the first large step toward fulfilling our vision of a global, ubiquitous timing utility."

The project was posted on the free market bulletin board, and the top engineers were recruited by management. According to Thirumale, a "crack" eight-member team of engineers was pulled together and delivered a proposal in about twelve days. The team then worked furiously to develop a prototype, which was also delivered on schedule at the end of February. The effort was a success: HP was selected as a finalist, and a few months later the division won the contract to start building the product.

Most employees viewed the Qualcomm project as a positive and critical step in the right direction and one that could not have come about without the redesign. One manager said, "The team did in less than three hundred hours what would normally have taken them three *years*. They pulled together, addressed issues, decided to go after it, and got a response back to the customer. They gave it everything they had. That's the pace we'll have to work at and the only way we are going to survive." An engineer explained: "Qualcomm would never have happened in the past because we couldn't respond fast enough. It was clearly a departure from the traditional way of doing business—a shift that would have never taken place in the old organization. That is purely driven from this new organization, aggressive posture, and SDBS strategy." A project manager familiar with the project said: "The redesign allowed us to act upon things like this Qualcomm deal in a timely fashion. Without the organizational change we wouldn't have acted on it as quickly. In the past something like Qualcomm would have been viewed as an interruption to the normal way of doing business."

1995: SIGNS OF SUCCESS

By mid-1995, more than three years after the redesign began, there were signs that the division was turning the corner. According to Neil, the SDBS team had met its revenue projections, and the division was producing the SmartClock in large quantities. Other large telecommunications customers were being lined up as well, and additional orders were expected by the end of the year. Neil explained: "A year ago, we didn't know what to work on. Eighty-five percent of our engineers were working on old stuff. But today, 85 percent our engineers are working on new timing and synchronization products and there is more business than we can handle! For the first time in years we're beginning to hire new people, and I anticipate that new jobs will grow between 8 and 10 percent in 1996." Employees' confidence, too, was on the rise. According to Neil, the division's 1995 survey revealed that over 80 percent of Santa Clara's employees agreed with the changes under way and believed that the division was moving in the right direction.

The existence of new projects provided opportunities to practice and strengthen many of the organization's new principles. For instance, as the number of new projects began to grow, the free market system began to operate, and engineers began choosing projects on which they wanted to work. Brandemuehl explained: "Engineers in the old business were anxious because they knew they were working on designs that would not be part of the division's future, and they were eager to work on the new designs. Now, the CSMs and program leaders hold meetings and pitch all the new projects, and engineers apply for jobs in a real-time way. The free market gave them a choice about finding a way to add value."

Over time, according to Neil and Brandemuehl, the majority of engineers had also become more comfortable working with customers. "They're continually experiencing more customer interface," said Neil. "It's still a stretch for them, but they are beginning to enjoy it." Giving teams of engineers ownership for projects had turned out to be effective. Brandemuehl explained: "When engineers are told they own particular customer accounts, they realize they need to figure out what resources they'll need, etc. Ultimately, they figure out that they'll be the ones going out on customer visits." According to Neil, the most effective way to get engineers to work with customers was to impress on them that there was no alternative. "We told them there was simply nobody else to do it," Neil explained somewhat sheepishly. He described one incident to illustrate his strategy: "We were designing a product for a large Korean electronics company. The customer over there found a bug in the prototype, so we had to go find out what was wrong. We also didn't want to lose the order. So we put an engineer on a plane and told him to go close the business. Sure enough, he rose to the challenge and did a great job! It's like he felt new muscles he'd never used before and had to work through the soreness to build them up. So engineers are discovering that they can work with customers and are finding that they can be successful at it." Brandemuehl elaborated, saying, "Everybody struggles, but they just have to experience it."

1996: FINANCIAL RECOVERY

By 1996, the division was well on its way to financial recovery. The Synchronization business had experienced continued growth, and the division was producing custom products in large quantities. Neil explained that "1996 has turned out to be a much stronger year than we ever guessed. We've actually had to hire seventy people to meet demand, and we've formed nearly thirty self-managing teams throughout the division.

Our revenue has grown by over 20 percent this year alone." In four years, the division had almost doubled its revenue and was producing more income than it had at its peak a decade earlier in 1985.

REFLECTIONS ON THE REDESIGN

In the years following the redesign, Neil and his staff reflected on the role that the redesign had played in SCD's transformation. Restructuring the division before a business strategy was in place had been risky, managers agreed, but necessary. Brandemuehl explained: "We were the classic case of an organization that was trying to change its strategy and its organization in parallel. That doesn't always work because while people always recognize the burning platform in the business strategy, they don't always recognize it in the organization. It was very hard to have a theoretical conversation with people about why we were changing when they didn't know exactly what the new strategy was going to be." But, Brandemuehl explained, they had no choice: "We knew that given the urgency of our business situation, improvements had to be made quickly. We started with the organization because it was causing so many barriers that it would prevent us from finding the right strategy."

Involving employees in the redesign had also been difficult, managers agreed, but vital. Neil explained: "The lack of knowledge individuals had about the business was amazing. At first, I was convinced that they would not be able to get the big picture quickly enough. It takes time for a set of folks to develop the breadth of perspective to understand what you're talking about. But when we gave them the room to go for it themselves, they rose to the occasion. It took longer, but they did it." Neil was more convinced than ever that shifting power and authority downward was critical to the division's survival. "I've found that turning management over to the workforce is crucial," he said. "I'm telling people that I'm not running the business—they are—because it results in faster decisions!"

Although much progress had been made in changing the division's inwardly turned, technology-driven culture to one that was outwardly focused and customer-driven, Neil said the cultural transformation was not yet complete—and had been far more difficult than finding a new business. Neil explained: "Our business direction, finding the theory of our business, that's over. But the second part, does the organization have the capacity, the skill sets, to thrive, we're not quite done there. Now that orders are coming in, responsiveness has become the number one organizational skill we need to have. We have to be able to prototype new products in weeks, ramp them up in a matter of months, and respond immediately to unforecasted demand. That's a completely different set of organizational skills than we've needed in the past. Being that responsive means decisions have to be made at lower levels—that's the reason for going to the high-performance team model. So changing the culture, moving toward the high-performance environment, and developing the organizational capacity remains the most difficult. Finding a new business direction was quicker; changing the culture is the hard part."

3 • CHANGING BY DESIGN

8 • REDESIGNING ORGANIZATIONS AS SYSTEMS

Let us now return to the beginning of our story. We saw how, like many companies today, two divisions of Hewlett-Packard were suddenly faced with intense competition and a turbulent, unpredictable environment to which they had to adapt if they were to survive. To remain competitive in the fast-paced computer industry, Roseville's managers had substantially to reduce the cost of producing motherboards and quadruple the center's production volume. Santa Clara's managers had to create entirely new businesses to make up for the loss of a stable market that had supported them for over thirty years but had suddenly vanished. Managers at both sites knew they would have to make fundamental changes in their organizations to regain their competitiveness. They redesigned their organizations following STS principles (a strategy that was compatible with the HP culture), which required aligning the social and technical dimensions of their organizations with customers' needs. Managers who had been steeped in the HP Way also knew that they had to gain the full commitment of their employees if they were to succeed. Both efforts succeeded and produced significant improvements in performance. What can be learned from these accounts? What implications do the Roseville and Santa Clara cases hold for other organizations that must transform themselves to succeed in a fast-paced, competitive environment?

The chief lessons to be learned are that organizations must be recognized as systems, and employees must be engaged in their transformation. Conceptualizing organizations as systems helps managers ensure that no stone is left unturned. Such a comprehensive view offered through a systems lens helps to guarantee that an organization's business processes, its structure, and its culture are aligned toward a common mission. And including employees in an analysis and redesign of their own organizations produces tangible gains in their knowledge and commitment to the new organizational design. When employees' learning translates into new behavior that is supported by a new organizational design, the result is a high-performance organization that has institutionalized the capacity to learn and can continuously adapt to a fast-moving environment.

In this final chapter, I review how these HP managers identified the changes that were needed in their organizations' structures, cultures, and policies to orient them toward their customers' needs. Managers included employees in each step of the analysis and redesign of their organizations' technical and social systems—a strategy that expanded employees' perspectives, generated a sense of ownership and commitment to the new design, and overcame many of the other problems that thwart most efforts at transformation. By investing in their employees' capacity to learn and including them in making the necessary changes, these managers reaffirmed a core HP belief—that if given the right tools, employees will do a good job—a philosophy that has translated into a formidable competitive advantage (Linden and Upbin, 1996).

Replacing mass production's hierarchical organizational structures, "command and control" management styles, and rigid production systems with flat, flexible, and participative systems requires changes in every dimension of an organization, from its structure to its culture. We have seen the weaknesses inherent in some of the most popular strategies to change organizations and their cultures which, when used alone, are inadequate to produce organizational flexibility. TQM, for example, encourages employee participation, but it produces only incremental change and usually fails fundamentally to alter either the organization's structure or its production system. Business Process Reengineering can achieve dramatic, short-term results by redesigning core business processes, but its weakness is that it assumes an organization can be successfully transformed by concentrating exclusively on its technical aspects. Because reengineering ignores the human side of an organization, it is not surprising that the process often alienates both managers and employees.

A more comprehensive view of the organization as a system makes it clear, however, that an organization is composed of interrelated parts, each of which may have to be fundamentally changed in order to become mutually reinforcing and to be aligned with an organization's business strategy. To overlook the relationships between the organization's structure, production system, or human element is to miss an opportunity to create lasting change. This is the basic premise of STS theory—that organizations contain at least two subsystems—a technical system (machines, technology, administrative procedures, tools, conveyances) and a social system (employees' and managers' assumptions, beliefs and behaviors, and the rules, policies, and procedures that govern people) and that both systems must be altered simultaneously so that the total system can express the best match between the two (Herrick, 1990).

Hewlett-Packard developed a tool to make these relationships explicit. Known as the Bull's-Eye, it helps managers conceptualize and redesign their organizations as systems. The Bull's-Eye typically divides organizations into three subsystems—business, technical, and social—represented by concentric rings. In larger organizations such as Santa Clara, a fourth ring representing the organization's structure may be added (see Figure 9). In the middle of the Bull's-Eye are two critical elements: an organization's mission or purpose (often represented by customers' needs) and an organization's vision (a statement of the desired organizational culture, or the organization's values). The next step is to analyze and design changes in each of the subsystems to align them with the organization's mission and values.

Using a systems perspective ensures that all dimensions of an organization are examined in relationship to each other and changed if necessary. For instance, as Roseville's managers began at the core of their Bull's-Eye and worked outward, they realized that the Surface Mount Center's customers and business had already been established by the CPCD. The center's 1991 business objective was to improve its manufacturing process by reducing production costs by 15 percent and decreasing production cycle time to less than one day. When the Roseville design team members analyzed the center's technical system, they found that it too was essentially fixed—although the machines could be used more efficiently, the technology was already state-of-the-art. Thus the only subsystem they could improve was the social system that governed how employees actually did their work.

Based on this diagnosis, which precluded altering either the business or the technical system, the social system became the primary focus of the redesign. The design team decided that the best way to achieve the center's business objective would be to develop self-managing teams that contained the necessary power, knowledge, authority, and information to make decisions on their own, ultimately eliminating an entire level of supervisors. (The supervisors would become coaches in the interim to help employees form self-managing teams. When they were no longer needed as coaches, they would find new positions in the division or elsewhere within HP.) Employees would be prepared to work in self-managing teams through training in subjects such as goal-setting, interpersonal relations, and statistical process control. As the design team pressed forward, its members discovered that a skill-based pay system had to be devised to reward employees for acquiring new skills. They also found that the standard employee evaluation system that ranked individuals against each other would have to be redesigned to reward team performance.

But not all redesign efforts unfold in such a linear manner. At Santa

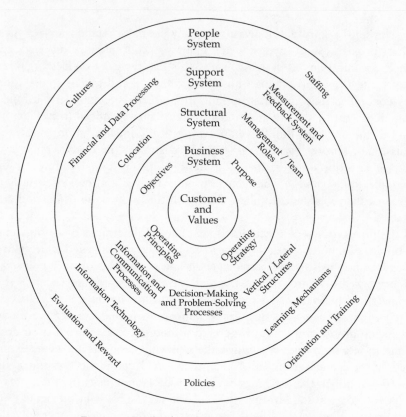

Figure 9. Santa Clara Division Bull's-Eye model

Clara, for example, the division's structure had to be completely dismantled before a business strategy could be established. The division's 1993 goal was clear, having been established by the parent test and measurement organization. Santa Clara would have to achieve a yearly growth of 10 percent in revenue and a 10 percent growth in net profit by 1997. Just how the division would achieve this goal, however, was far from clear. After twenty years of steady growth, managers had become complacent and had failed to notice that the division's business had changed irrevocably. The defense industry had all but disappeared, and competition for non-defense-related products had intensified. Moreover, customers wanted complete, integrated solutions to their problems rather than the division's general-purpose instruments. Santa Clara's Marty Neil knew that entirely new customers and businesses would have to be found before the division could possibly establish a business strategy that could produce over 10 percent annual profitable growth.

Neil's initial analysis of the division's business, technical, and social systems, however, revealed a troubling dilemma. The complexity of the division's businesses had created a structure that prevented the division from responding to the environment. As Neil commented, not only was Santa Clara in the wrong business, it had the wrong organization. Business decisions were supposed to be made by business teams made up of midlevel managers from the marketing, R&D, and manufacturing functions. These teams had the knowledge to make business decisions, but they did not have the authority, which rested with the management staff. When the business teams and the management staff could not agree, decisions were either postponed indefinitely—or decisions were made that optimized the division's R&D, marketing, and manufacturing functions rather than the business. Neil was convinced that the division would have to be fundamentally redesigned if decision making was to improve.

In the months that followed, the old organizational structure was demolished, and the division was reorganized around its businesses, or "customer segments." Each customer segment would be headed by business teams that would have both the knowledge and the authority to make decisions. Two new cross-functional processes (new product and process services and order fulfillment) were created to cut across the traditional functions (marketing, R&D, and manufacturing) contained in the vertical silos. Once this initial restructuring was complete, Neil and his new business managers agreed on a three-pronged business strategy. First, in a radical departure from its past, the division would step beyond its traditional test and measurement charter and enter the unpredictable and fast-growing global communications industry. Second, managers and engineers would reengineer the new product development process, the most complex of the four processes, to reduce the time and cost of getting products to market. Finally, managers and engineers would create a new organizational design that would reorient the division's culture. In this new design, engineers would take on more responsibility for running the division's businesses, become more accountable for financial results, and work more closely with customers to develop new products.

In 1993, Neil and his managers decided on a new business that would position the division as a player in the burgeoning telecommunications industry. Neil also formed a new product development (NPD) team to reengineer the new product development process and a transition team to devise a new internal structure that would empower engineers by giving them responsibility for entire businesses. The transition team also developed a new free market system that enabled engineers to plan ahead and select the projects they would work on.

Changes were made in some of the division's policies to support its new structure and culture. A critical policy change was a modification in the way R&D engineers were evaluated to encourage them to meet deadlines. They would no longer be evaluated simply on the extent of their research; now they would be evaluated and rewarded based on their contributions to the division's orders and profit.[1] Regular midcourse project reviews would be held each quarter, rather than only when a project was completed, to take stock of the project's status and to enable engineers to make adjustments in schedules and resources. Postproject reviews would become a standard practice so that project teams could learn from their mistakes. Finally, the design team investigated the possibility of ranking entire teams, rather than individuals, to encourage teamwork.

Over time, the division's culture underwent a slow but discernible shift. As engineers' beliefs and assumptions slowly began to change, they began to take more responsibility for meeting deadlines, and they showed a willingness to work in self-managing teams. Most important, as engineers became comfortable working with customers, they began to realize that it did not diminish the value of technology. Together, these changes helped the division begin to develop a culture that was outwardly focused and far more responsive to customers' needs than it had been in the past.

---

1. As Brandemuehl explained, however, employees would not be evaluated solely on whether their projects met their proposed deadlines. Other factors, such as whether the project was "high risk" or meeting the commitment was out of engineers' control, would be taken into account.

9 • HARNESSING HUMAN POTENTIAL

While systems theory is a critical first step in identifying elements of an organization that need to be changed, many of the changes can be mandated by management and completed in relatively short order. For example, departments can be relocated, reporting relationships can be redrawn, core processes can be reengineered, and new policies can be instituted. What cannot be mandated, however, are changes in the underlying beliefs and assumptions that managers and employees hold about the company and about each other that constitute an organization's culture. Indeed, changing employees' beliefs and behavior is the hardest part of all, and it is a leading reason why most change efforts fail (Peters and Waterman, 1982). Exchanging new beliefs for old ones and then translating the new beliefs into new behaviors is never accomplished easily. Such fundamental changes in patterns of thinking, however, are critical in order to harness peoples' potential and turn it into a competitive advantage (Pfeffer, 1994; Wilms, 1996).

PREREQUISITES TO CHANGE

Several prerequisites must exist before employees can become willing to take on more responsibility for decision making, work as a team, and learn a broader range of tasks. For example, they must feel a sense of security, or at least that they will be treated fairly. They must also feel that they can trust their managers and fellow employees and that they will be compensated for their efforts (Levine, 1990; Pfeffer, 1994). Such values have long been at the core of the HP Way, which David Packard and William Hewlett set forth as a foundation for the company. The HP Way is based on the belief that people *want* to do a good job and will do so if given the right environment and tools. The philosophy also insists that employees are to be treated with trust and respect and that their achievements are recognized. Employees share in the company's success through generous stock purchase plans and profit sharing, which ranges from just over 4 to almost 10 percent of employees' base salary (Packard, 1995). The company has never had a union.

A key element in harnessing employees' commitment is ensuring that they feel secure or at least that they will be treated fairly (Ouchi, 1981; Wilms, 1996). Hewlett-Packard has always placed a strong emphasis on providing employment security, and even though it is not a stated policy, this practice has usually been followed. At Roseville, managers, engineers, and supervisors were willing to let production operators take over their responsibilities and in some cases eliminate their jobs entirely because they knew they would not be laid off when their jobs disappeared. When it truly became necessary to reduce staff at both sites, employees were demoralized but knew that HP would do everything possible to find them another job—if not at the same site, at another HP division that was growing. Roseville's supervisors found jobs in other parts of the division, and some engineers at Santa Clara transferred to the computer side of the company or to HP Labs. When such opportunities cannot be found, HP makes necessary reductions in its workforce through early retirements and a program of voluntary severance, under which employees who are willing to leave are offered a generous financial package. Thus, though downsizing will inevitably reduce employee morale, companies like HP can ensure that employees still feel fairly treated by doing everything possible to find them a job elsewhere.

Trust is another prerequisite to employees' willingness to take on more responsibility and authority and to work as a team (Fukuyama, 1995). For example, when Roseville section manager Steve Tracy withheld information about the center's possible consolidation to prevent employees from becoming anxious, they concluded the worst—that the rumors they had heard were true and the center was about to be shut down. Their anxiety turned to distrust when they further assumed that Tracy was unconcerned about their futures. Once Tracy realized what had happened, he resolved to share *all* information with employees, even if the news was bad. Lack of trust between employees themselves can also thwart teamwork. At Roseville, teamwork became impossible when Caucasian production operators assumed the Filipino workers' desires to group together because of their common culture and language was separatism, while the Filipinos interpreted the Caucasians' reactions as discriminatory. Only when these perceptions were aired and employees could resolve to bridge the gap by establishing English-language classes and courses in interpersonal relations did employees become willing to work as a team.

THE COMPLEXITY OF SHARING POWER

Creating an organization that can respond quickly in a fast-moving environment requires that decision-making power rests not only in the hands of managers but also in the hands of employees who control the means of production and who are closest to customers' changing preferences. But relinquishing power at the top and placing it further down in an organization is difficult because it requires a cultural change. Managers who have been accustomed to controlling employees must overcome generations of conditioning and be willing to share their power. Employees, in turn, must become willing to take on more decision-making power and responsibility. But, as we have seen, even in a company like HP that values autonomy and individual contribution, making this cultural transition is far more difficult than it may seem.

Most of the managers leading the redesign efforts at both HP sites were willing to share their power because they truly believed that giving employees more responsibility for designing and controlling their work was the only way their organizations would survive. As Hendrickson explained, the best way to create a sense of ownership and responsibility was to have employees create the new work system themselves, rather than have it be imposed on them by managers. Steve Tracy convinced the Roseville design team members that he was willing to relinquish his own authority so thoroughly that they surprised him with a list of his new "menial" activities: he would take make the coffee, take out the trash, mop the floor, and park the cars. The list was a joke, but it symbolized a new relationship between Tracy and the team. In his new job as business manager, Tracy's focus would no longer be to manage the center—that would be done by the employees. Tracy would be in charge of strategic planning and would look beyond the center to find new business opportunities. Similarly, Santa Clara division manager Marty Neil not only advocated pushing power and responsibility downward, he did it. Murli Thirumale, one of Santa Clara's new business managers, who insisted that engineers rather than managers be the ones to talk to customers, explained that empowerment is no longer just a "nice thing to do"; it is now a business imperative.

The process of exchanging power is complex and requires that managers strike a balance between giving up enough control to enable employees to make decisions but retain enough power to prevent employees from feeling abandoned and to lead an organization in a common direction. At Santa Clara, for instance, Neil knew he had to give the transition team control over the internal structure of the division, but he felt intense pressure to complete the restructuring as soon as possible so that managers could turn their attention to creating new businesses. He also had his own ideas about how the internal structure should work and felt pressure from his own steering committee, half of which opposed handing control over to the team. Caught in a dilemma, Neil reasoned that if he did not relinquish power, his employees would distrust him because he would fail to model the very behavior he advocated. If he gave employees full control over designing the division's internal structure, however, he ran the risk that the team would reject his suggestions and come up with their own ideas, which could take months and still might not produce the best answer. As events turned out, Neil and his managers were able to strike a reasonably good balance between giving up and retaining power to enable the team to make their own decisions, although some engineers grumbled that they had been "handed the right answer."

At the other extreme, abdicating power too quickly can have negative consequences. At the Roseville Center, Steve Tracy purposely stayed off the production floor, thinking that by minimizing his presence, he would encourage the development of self-managing teams. Instead, Tracy's absence made employees feel that they had been forgotten and that Tracy no longer cared about the center or appreciated their hard work. Employees pointed out that like their peers in surrounding departments, they too wanted to be recognized when they achieved their production goals.

Pushing power downward in an organization can precipitate other unforeseen events that become hard to manage. And trying to retrieve power once given up may be impossible or may incur substantial cost. For instance, Hendrickson found that as design team members began exercising their newfound power, they became more vocal and began to question the authority of supervisors and engineers and even of HP corporate executives. For example, production operators shocked the Center's engineers when they told them they could not stop the line to conduct experiments because it would disrupt production. The design team members also suggested changes to HP's corporate-wide policies that Hendrickson knew made sense but would be nearly impossible to make. For instance, they suggested changing HP's long-standing practice of ranking individuals based on a normal curve distribution because they felt it discouraged teamwork. Hendrickson likened employees' discovery of their newfound power to "letting the tiger out of the cage," which she knew could not be put back. She predicted that if managers tried to revert back to the way things were, there would be "mass regression."

Most research studies conclude that managers and supervisors have the most difficulty in giving up power (Klein, 1984). Conversely, studies also show that employees are usually eager to take on a broader range of tasks and responsibilities and to exercise more discretion in their work. Indeed, at Roseville, most production operators welcomed the opportunity to expand their skills and to participate in decisions about their work. As Hendrickson explained, when she talked with the center's employees about the concept of working in self-managing teams, they loved the idea and saw redesign as a way to create it. Throughout the entire redesign experience, the design team members expressed intense enthusiasm, often working well into the evenings. Employees described experiencing feelings of euphoria with their new roles and responsibilities. Some said it was like being on a "high."

Findings from this study show, however, that not all employees easily embrace new responsibilities and authority. This was especially true of the R&D engineers at Santa Clara who, as "knowledge workers," already held positions of status and power. The goals of the redesign calling for all employees to become more customer-focused, broadly skilled, accountable for results, and flexible were initially disdained by most engineers. Other engineers regarded them as downright undesirable.[1] Although engineers who volunteered to work on the redesign wanted the division to survive, most participated out of a sense of "civic duty," not because they were willing to give up their power and authority. R&D engineers had always enjoyed the highest status among their fellow workers. They were called the "kings of the hill" and naturally had little incentive to give up their privileged position. Most of the R&D engineers loved technology and had little desire to do anything but advance knowledge. As one engineer said bluntly, he came to Santa Clara to do circuit design, not to talk on the phone with customers. This was more than surface-level emotion because becoming customer-focused threatened the very foundations of the prestige and status engineers had enjoyed for decades. A customer focus was interpreted by many of the engineers as a loss of independence because, under the new organizational design, customers' preferences would take precedence over their own judgment. Engineers also resisted being held accountable for meeting deadlines, arguing that R&D was a creative and unpredictable process that was impossible to standardize. "I can't invent on a schedule" was a familiar refrain. Bringing about the necessary behavioral changes among members of this group, let alone producing deeper cultural changes, would be extraordinarily difficult. First, it would require that management dismantle the old R&D organization to convey the message that engineers could no longer work in isolation from other departments or from customers' desires. It would also require that engineers truly un-

---

1. I do not mean to imply that all production operators at Roseville wanted to become empowered. Indeed, a small proportion resisted taking on more responsibility. But the magnitude of resistance was nowhere near that at Santa Clara.

derstand the need to change and that they be given some ownership over the change process. Finally, it would require that engineers have opportunities to learn new behaviors through experience and that new incentives be crafted to reward their achievements.

LEARNING BY DESIGN

But simply pushing power and authority downward into the organization is not enough to develop the necessary organizational flexibility and responsiveness. Working as self-managing teams, scheduling production runs, finding defects and the root causes of problems, and interacting with customers requires greater knowledge and skills, as well as higher levels of motivation and commitment than most front-line employees possessed. Having included employees on the design teams, managers were faced with the immediate challenge of teaching them the necessary knowledge and skills to complete the redesign quickly enough so that their organizations could survive.

As managers would discover, the answer lay in the redesign process itself. The detailed and intensive process of doing the business, technical, and social analyses proved to be a powerful tool for learning. Discovering customers' needs firsthand and benchmarking their organization against their competitors helped employees develop a clear understanding of just how competitive HP's markets had become and how much their own center would have to improve to become competitive. Participating in the technical analysis at Roseville revealed the value of employees' contribution. It taught production operators how to streamline their production line and use Statistical Process Control further to improve its efficiency, and conveyed the need to work in self-managing teams. Similarly, engineers at Santa Clara learned about the urgency of improving the division's ROI by hearing Neil describe the division's dire business situation. They learned how to work cooperatively across functions to speed up the way new products were chosen and developed, and how to establish realistic project time lines to which they would be held accountable. Participating in the social analysis taught employees how their own beliefs and assumptions influenced their behavior, conveyed the importance of the division's new values, and helped them reexamine the HP culture in light of changing external demands. Now let us review how this learning actually occurred.

Broadening Perspectives

Traditionally, employees know very little about their own organization's business: how their company compares to its competitors or the identity of their company's customers and their preferences. In the absence of such knowledge, employees lack the means—and often the motivation—to think about much more than their own limited jobs. When management announces new initiatives to improve quality or productivity, employees, limited by this narrow vision, often perceive them as "just another program." Thus they view them with skepticism and distrust and predict their early demise. We saw evidence, however, that including employees in redesigning their own organizations helps to overcome this skepticism and conveys the urgency of the need to change. For example, at Roseville, design team members who worked on the business analysis learned firsthand from customers that their costs were too high to be competitive. They also learned that their customers expected better quality and faster responsiveness to their requirements for different models of products. As the design team members expanded their view of the center's business, they had little doubt that they had to improve. Even though their customers were right across the aisle in the same building, members never knew what PC Assembly expected from the center and were shocked to learn that poor product quality was their number one complaint. A design team member admitted that she became interested in finding out who the center's customers were and what they wanted only after she got off the line and interviewed them. As Santa Clara's engineers were drawn into planning with top management, their horizons began to widen and they began to grasp the division's grave business situation, a necessary first step toward change. Engineers heard from Thirumale that the division had been called slow, arrogant, bureaucratic, and inflexible, which hit home when Neil shared with engineers the division's dwindling orders and meager sales figures. Engineers began to realize that unless they built products that customers wanted, the division would not be around much longer to build *anything*.

Only when employees understood the larger business situations facing their organizations could they understand how and why they personally would need to change. To explain why engineers would have to talk to customers directly, Thirumale used the metaphor of the telephone game to illustrate how information invariably becomes garbled when it passes from the customer through managers and finally to engineers. Managers must be taken out of the middle, Thirumale explained, to avoid distorting technical information that engineers needed to create customized products. Thirumale also used real-life situations to convey how engineers' lack of business understanding translates into slow decisionmaking. Through examples such as these, engineers gradually understood how and why they needed to change. Eventually, many came to understand that unless they took on more responsibility for running existing businesses to give managers more time to find new ones, the division probably would not survive.

Once employees had been convinced of the need to change, including them in the technical analysis helped to expand their vision of the entire production process and their role in it. As production workers and engineers carefully traced the flow of products from their initial design through production to sales, they began to grasp the value of their contribution to every step of the process. Roseville's production operators explained that before the redesign, they focused only on their own areas and cared little about how the line functioned as a whole. After the redesign, they understood the impact of their work on employees downstream and began troubleshooting up the line to find the cause of problems. After Santa Clara's engineers traced projects through the R&D and marketing functions and measured the time and cost of each step, they understood for the first time how the antiquated organization and their self-interested behavior led to increased costs and missed deadlines. R&D engineers learned how their common practice of agreeing to whatever managers wanted to avoid feeling pressured actually caused projects to be over budget and behind schedule by a factor of two. Engineers also learned how poor communication between R&D and marketing led to widespread ignorance about actual due dates for projects and just how late they usually were.

Obtaining Commitment

One of the reasons that classical Business Process Reengineering has had such limited success is that it separates the design of work from its execution. Like mass production, it ignores the human element and treats employees, as Thomas Davenport, one of the creators of reengineering, said, as "so many bits and bytes, interchangeable parts to be reengineered" (1995a:71). Clearly, as long as employees are regarded simply as extensions of their machines, they will have no motivation to assume any sense of ownership and responsibility for the enterprise.

In the case of these two HP divisions, however, a strong sense of ownership and an enormous commitment to the redesign effort were produced by including employees in the act of creating a new organizational design. For example, production operators at Roseville stood back and cheered after they had successfully redesigned their assembly line. After witnessing such a display of ownership and pride, there was little doubt that taking over control of their production system was a significant step toward employee empowerment. Employees' sense of commitment to the design, they explained, also helped them overcome intense anxiety they felt before presenting it to a group of managers. Operators who admitted that they were "nervous as hell" about speaking before others, let alone managers, quelled their fears by reasoning with themselves that if they were confident in their new design, they should be able to explain it to others, regardless of who they were. Their logic worked, and they presented their report smoothly, providing clear evidence that these employees owned the design they had produced. Employees at Santa Clara became committed to the new organization in another, related way. Engineers on the design team who had devised the new free market system successfully convinced their peers that it would give them more say in which projects the division chose to pursue and more choice over the projects they worked on. Worries that "MBA-minded managers" would select short-term projects at the expense of longer-term investments in technology began to abate when engineers realized that, in the new structure, empowered teams of engineers, not managers, would choose the technologies to develop.

Cultural Obstacles to Change

One of the reasons that Business Process Reengineering is often unable to produce lasting positive change is that it fails to raise the underlying cultural factors—employees' underlying assumptions and beliefs—that, if left unacknowledged, often doom the implementation of a new organizational design. Including employees in reengineering their own work processes can overcome many of these cultural obstacles. At Roseville, for instance, discussion of the multiple meanings of the word "team" revealed how its use could actually undermine teamwork by pitting teams of production operators against each other in unhealthy competition. By substituting the word "group," the language could be aligned with the culture and the effectiveness of the new design was improved. In another example, a production operator watched his peers redesign his job from the high-tech, high-status, front end of the line to the lower-status rear end of the line. He momentarily resisted but then agreed because, through the redesign process, he had gained trust in his peers and had come to understand and accept that the new arrangement was for the greater good of the center. Had this operator not been included in the redesign and suddenly found that his job had been moved, his resistance no doubt would have been far greater. Similarly, at Santa Clara, because they had been included in the redesign process, the engineers on both the new product development and the transition teams were able to identify a host of thorny issues that would likely have been overlooked by managers. For instance, engineers explained their resistance to being held accountable for deadlines when certain steps in the product development process were out of their control. Like the production operators at Roseville, they explained that the use of the word "teamwork" sounded to them like a "management ploy" to get them to volunteer for jobs they did not want. Engineers were also able honestly to describe their managers' tendencies to promote and invest huge sums in large, potentially lucrative projects over smaller, though potentially important ones, as well as how project managers used their power to squelch ideas they did not like. In each of these cases, raising human issues that would have remained invisible in top-down reengineering efforts—and might have thwarted the attempt to change—served as instrumental forms of learning that helped align the division's culture with its business objective.

TRANSLATING LEARNING INTO NEW BEHAVIORS

For learning to be useful, however, it must translate into new behaviors that help organizations become more competitive. Indeed, when learning occurs without changing the way work is done, only the *potential* for improvement exists (Garvin, 1993). In some cases, learning translates naturally into behavioral change. For example, once production operators at Roseville learned about their customers' needs and had the opportunity to expand their skills and scope of authority, they began making decisions as a team rather than looking to their supervisor for direction. They began scheduling production and deciding whether to work overtime—decisions that until then had remained solely in the hands of managers. When employees detected technical problems on the line, they would shut the line down themselves and go straight to an engineer for help rather than consult their supervisor. One manager explained that this behavior was unheard-of before the redesign, even at HP. Employees also began venturing beyond the boundaries of their own work areas to find the root causes of problems. Documenting the entire production process and becoming cross-trained enabled employees to learn each others' jobs, raising everyone's level of knowledge and investment. Commenting on how employees' motivation increased, a manager joked, "They're acting like they own the place!"

Similar behavioral changes took place among the engineers in Santa Clara as they learned to work in self-managing teams. Engineers on the first self-managing team devised project checklists to ensure that they overlooked no steps in developing new products and also learned to share the stress that came with their new accountability. Engineers enjoyed the feeling that they could tolerate more ambiguity and take on more responsibility because they were "united."

Not all changes, however, were as easy for the engineers. Bringing about some desired changes required more than intellectual understanding to overcome resistance to change.

OVERCOMING RESISTANCE TO CHANGE

Intellectual understanding is not always enough to produce behavioral change, especially when there is resistance to the desired new behaviors. As we saw at Santa Clara, while engineers adapted relatively easily to working in self-managing teams and to being more accountable for business deadlines, getting engineers to work with customers in the product design phase was far harder to achieve. Some engineers outright refused the notion of becoming "customer-driven" because it was antithetical to the value they placed on advancing technology, and it also threatened the high-status positions they had enjoyed for decades. Even those engineers who agreed intellectually with the need to talk to customers resisted actually doing so, and they would give themselves every possible excuse to avoid picking up the telephone and calling customers or going to visit them. Some engineers feared appearing ignorant when customers talked about areas with which they were unfamiliar. Many resisted the notion of having to "sell" their ideas, thinking that the excellence of their products should speak for itself. Still others dreaded the responsibility of having to carry on conversations with customers, especially when customers were not talkative.

Overcoming engineers' resistance to working with customers would require learning through experience that was bolstered by strong incentives to change. A powerful first step, Brandemuehl explained, was to tell engineers, "You own this project." They would then apply their skills of logic and precision to managing the project and eventually face the reality that they would have to go out to visit customers. Santa Clara's division manager Neil confirmed that the most successful strategy for getting engineers to talk to customers was telling them that there was simply nobody else to do it. Once engineers experienced working with customers, he explained, most admitted that it was not as bad as they had anticipated. And once engineers realized that they were actually good at it, talking to customers became a positive experience rather than a negative one.

When I last talked to Neil and Brandemuehl in 1996, they said that while not all engineers found it easy, the majority had been able to overcome their initial resistance and to work successfully with customers. Several engineers I spoke with concurred. One individual who several years earlier had refused to go on customer visits spoke with pride when he said, "I've seen more customers in the last year than I have in my entire career with HP!" A key to engineers' success, it turned out, was getting over their initial anxiety by finding common ground to discuss with customers. Most often, the topic that opened the door to the beginning of a relationship was technology. As one engineer explained, the hardest part of talking to customers is the first few minutes. Once he and the customer start talking "shop," the discussion becomes second nature.

INSTITUTIONALIZING NEW BEHAVIORS

Often, organizations embark on efforts to change the way employees work—for instance, by teaching them how to identify and reduce waste or how to work in self-managing teams—that initially result in behavioral change. These new behaviors typically fail to last, however, because they are not reinforced (Lawler, 1991). Including employees in redesigning their organizations as systems helps to institutionalize the new behaviors by making changes in an organization's structure, policies, and practices that support the new patterns of working. For example, the production operators at Roseville knew that it would be impossible to work in self-managing teams under HP's existing ranking system, which forced employees' performance into a normal distribution, thus rating individuals against each other and creating unhealthy competition. Team members decided to replace the individual-based ranking system with one that would evaluate team productivity. The new emphasis on initiative and empowerment led the Santa Clara team to create a free market system to institutionalize the process of participating in choosing projects on which they wanted to work. To reinforce the new emphasis on accountability, the evaluation system was modified so that engineers were evaluated not on how hard they worked but on whether they met project deadlines and impacted the business.[2] In this way, changes to each site's policies and practices help reinforce, and in some cases encourage, the emergence of new behaviors.

TRANSLATING NEW BEHAVIORS INTO ORGANIZATIONAL PERFORMANCE

Even if these new behaviors are successfully institutionalized, they must translate into improved organizational performance for work redesign to become a competitive advantage (Mohrman and Mohrman, 1989). In other words, the true test of any strategy to change an organization is whether it produces results. At both sites we saw evidence that employees' learning produced significant, tangible improvements in organizational performance. Even before the new organizational design was implemented, Roseville's employees discovered more than one hundred variances in the production system, which, when controlled, reduced production costs by

2. The transition team had not yet redesigned the evaluation system so this initiative came from managers.

15 percent. These immediate gains were achieved simply by teaching employees how to find variances in the production line and giving them the freedom to do it.

Even more important, the new behaviors must translate in the long term into an organization's ability to adapt to fast-paced business environments. Here the value of investing in employees' capacity to learn becomes most apparent because it is through broader learning, rather than narrow skills training, that employees become able to respond to new situations. As Roseville's production manager explained, it was the process of having the team conduct a business, technical, and social analysis, not the new design itself, that created lasting value and changed the way operators perceived their jobs. Roseville's redesign aimed to increase employees' knowledge and flexibility by teaching them how to interpret changes in the business environment and how to respond by adjusting their organizations accordingly. The success of this strategy became apparent when employees' learning acquired during the first redesign saved the center from being shut down and enabled it to be transformed once again.

The story of the center's transformation is particularly instructive as an example of how investing in employees' ability to learn can translate into an organization's ability to adapt to a changing environment. Just as the center was about to be closed as part of HP's personal computer strategy, managers from a neighboring division visited the center to find out how it was able to produce such high-quality boards while reducing production costs by 25 percent. They were surprised to learn that these improvements had come about not through new technology but as the result of employees' increased knowledge of the business and broader range of skills that enabled them to be more flexible. These managers quickly recognized the value of the center's highly committed and capable employees and decided to adopt the center as their own, rather than have it shut down. To fulfill its new role, the center would have to redesign itself from a manufacturing organization to one that developed and built prototype motherboards. Though the newly designed center would require only one-fifth of its original workforce, those employees who remained with the center—many of whom had been on the design team—were able to apply what they had learned from the first redesign to guide the center through a second redesign that enabled it to perform its new role with astonishingly high speed and quality. Within the first eight weeks, the center was able to prototype an unprecedented thirty-five boards, doubling managers' expectations. Production Manager Dennis Early was convinced that without the knowledge employees gained during the first redesign, the second redesign would have been impossible. Early praised the new and high-performing organization and said it was like having the "engine all tuned up," in that once the center was in its new home, employees immediately went to work analyzing its new business requirements and redesigning their new production system to enable the center to practice its new charter successfully.

Santa Clara's redesign produced equally as impressive improvements in the division's performance and its ability to respond to the environment. The first self-managing team that formed to pilot the division's new "Sell-Design-Build-Support" strategy learned to work smoothly without a project manager and to work with customers in defining new products. By the end of 1994, the team had met its targets to design and sell six custom hardware packages and to produce millions of dollars in revenue. Similarly, a team that formed to develop a proposal for a large telecommunications customer did so in record time and won the contract to build the product. By late 1995, the division was producing the SmartClock in large quantities for a growing number of well-known telecommunications customers and had successfully introduced the product overseas. Nearly thirty self-managing teams had formed throughout the division, and 85 percent of its engineers were working on new products. By 1996 the division had more projects than it could handle and had hired new employees to help meet the growing demand for its products.

REMAINING OBSTACLES TO WORK REDESIGN

STS redesign is clearly not a panacea or a magical solution for any company that is being forced to change. The concept has been in existence since the late 1950s, but its use has remained limited because it is extremely difficult to do and until recently has not been necessary. Companies instead have preferred to adopt more rational and controllable approaches to organizational improvement such as TQM and Business Process Reengineering. STS redesign differs in two main ways. First, it views an organization as a system that may have to be pulled up by its roots to bring its structure, core processes, and culture into alignment. Second, redesign maintains that the only way to create an organization that can respond to its environment is to give employees the power and authority to create and control their own work systems. Only in this way can an organization benefit from employees' expertise and obtain their commitment to a new work structure.

There are at least four reasons why these principles make STS redesign extremely difficult to do. First, redesign requires an extraordinary commitment from managers who lead the effort. Second, it takes considerable time and human energy, and many organizations find they cannot afford to invest the necessary time and resources to conduct a full-blown redesign in a fast-paced environment. Third, enabling learning to extend beyond the design team to the larger workforce presents a difficult problem. Finally, sustaining redesign efforts, especially when they occur within larger organizations that are not part of the redesign, also presents challenges.

Inadequate Leadership

Strong leadership at the top of an organization is a critical ingredient to bringing about a successful organizational transformation (Beer and Walton, 1990). Top management must be willing fundamentally to alter all dimensions of an organization, which involves great risk. One year into the redesign, Santa Clara division manager Marty Neil said, "We didn't do this redesign to tinker with the organization. We did it out of desperation. We wouldn't have embarked on this otherwise, because it scared the hell out of me." Top management must also be truly committed to pushing power and authority downward and must model the behavior it advocates if those at lower levels are to become truly empowered. Neil, for example, was truly convinced that enabling teams of engineers to take on responsibility for working with customers and for running projects was the only way the division would survive. Indeed, as he turned management responsibilities over to the workforce, he found that decisions were made much more quickly. Rather than select the new customer segment managers and program leaders himself, he assembled selection committees made up of managers and employees who interviewed and hired their own new bosses.

Not all managers, however, are comfortable with shifting authority downward or with developing the "softer" elements of skill, values, and leadership (Beer and Eisenstat, 1996). Hendrickson, who coached the managers through Roseville's redesign process, explained: "They buy into it intellectually. But for them to get in there and roll up their sleeves and interact on a personal level with employees . . . we're not there." She explained why redesign was hard for many managers: "If they're not comfortable with the human issues, redesign seems like touchy-feely, hocus-pocus stuff that can make managers feel very uncomfortable." Because redesign requires raising peoples' underlying beliefs and assumptions, it can seem very irrational to many managers, especially those with engineering backgrounds who are more comfortable dealing with scientific methods. As Steve Tracy, Roseville's section manager explained, redesign is also difficult because it requires giving up control, which is very difficult for American managers.

Redesign's Lengthy Cycle Time

Even when managers are fully committed to a redesign and are able to share their power and authority, they must find ways to conduct the redesign quickly enough for the organization to survive. According to some estimates, it takes eighteen months to complete work redesign (Macy, Izumi, Bliese, and Norton, 1993). At Roseville, the redesign process took nearly seven months, but even that was too long. Just as the new design was being implemented, it was rendered obsolete by a change in the center's business strategy. Roseville's managers began to recognize that the traditional redesign process, which was well adapted to a slower-paced environment, could not keep up in the turbulent 1990s. As Roseville production manager Dennis Early explained, the turbulent environment almost "outstripped" the center's ability to change. While managers were aware of the need to "renew" the redesign even as it was being implemented, they had not anticipated facing change so radical that the redesign process could not keep up. Other managers noted that to keep up with this pace of change, the center would need to redesign itself in a matter of weeks. Hendrickson joked, "To keep up in this environment, we need people who can change and change fast—like turbo-chameleons!"

Santa Clara's managers also discovered that the redesign process took too long. The transition team had been given three months to design a new internal structure for the division, and this deadline could not be extended. Ten weeks into the process, the transition team still had to conduct the social analysis and to redesign the division's pay, evaluation, and training systems. The engineers on the team were exasperated with the amount of work and with the frantic pace and said they would need at least twenty more hours per week to feel good about their contribution to the redesign. To complete its proposal on time, the team was forced to shortcut the process by outsourcing the social analysis to our UCLA research team and to postpone decisions about employee evaluations, rewards, incentives, and training to a later date. As one member explained, even though he did not feel "educated enough," he realized the team had to move on. Even after truncating the process, the design team still required twelve hundred hours to complete its proposal, more than double the amount of time that had been allotted. Neil was stunned at the amount of time that had been invested in the effort and worried because he knew that redesigning the division's pay, evaluation, and training systems would probably take at least as long.

Evidence from this study confirms that a first redesign is usually lengthy because employees have to learn how to analyze and redesign an organization as a system. After employees and managers have internalized these skills and abilities, however, subsequent redesigns may be accomplished far more quickly. One Roseville manager said he did not fault the lengthiness of the redesign because he believed that much of what occurred was actually teaching the organization how to learn. He speculated that if the design team were to do another redesign in production, it could be done in weeks.

There was truth in his observation as members of the redesign team were able to apply what they learned to a second, cross-functional redesign to transform the center from a manufacturing shop to a prototype shop in record time. The engineers at Santa Clara also acknowledged that learning how to redesign an organization had been a long, arduous process. They assured Neil, however, that they could accomplish subsequent redesigns much more quickly.

In a more stable environment, redesign could be regarded as a means to solve problems, but in today's dynamic environment it must be a continuous process to help organizations adapt and learn from change. Lyman Ketchum, who introduced work redesign to the highly successful General Foods pet food plant in Topeka, Kansas, recognized that work redesign is a continuous process of learning and change. He noted, "Work redesign is a system-wide, long-term process of assessing and planning change, trying it, learning from it, and then repeating the process" (1981:85). Once managers and employees have learned how to execute a successful redesign, their expertise becomes internalized and redesign may become a continuous process rather than a onetime event. Santa Clara transition manager Jenny Brandemuehl said that the changing environment made her and the division's managers realize that redesign was going to become a long-term, ongoing change effort. Similarly, Roseville's Kathy Hendrickson acknowledged that she had wrongly viewed their work redesign as a onetime effort. Instead, she had learned that redesign must be done quickly and must be viewed as a cyclical process, not as a project that one can start and stop.

Transferring Learning

Another dilemma is how to extend the learning that flows from conducting the business, technical, and social analyses from a small design team to a larger group, or a "critical mass" of employees. Kathy Hendrickson anticipated the difficulty of replicating such intense learning among members of the larger Surface Mount Center workforce. She tried to create a learning experience for them by engaging the entire workforce in a search for variances in the production system as part of the technical analysis. In a more ambitious effort to help foster learning among the workforce, she bused all 140 employees to a local fairgrounds, where she led them through a week-long, though abbreviated, redesign effort she called Summer School. But even though it was carefully constructed to prepare employees to work in self-managing teams, this condensed redesign did not reproduce the intense learning and the resulting commitment experienced by the original design team members. As one frustrated design team member explained, he tried to convince the workforce of the value of working in self-managing teams, only to realize that his peers would have to experience it for themselves. In a similar way, Santa Clara division manager Marty Neil tried to galvanize the division's employees into action by holding special coffee talks during which he and other managers explained the division's dire business situation and need to become more responsive to customers' needs. Engineers on the design team also held special luncheons with their peers and walked the aisles, talking to engineers in an effort to convince them of the redesign's potential. But this was only talk; in the absence of proof of the redesign's value and without the intense experience to change peoples' beliefs and behaviors, much of the workforce initially remained skeptical about the proposed changes because they were not involved in creating them.

The problem of transferring learning more quickly may be at least partially solved by new large-group methodologies that are now emerging such as future-search conferences and participative redesign, which HP divisions have already begun to use. These techniques aim to extend the educational benefits to larger populations beyond initial design teams, and can also be conducted in shorter periods of time.[3] Future-search conferences, created by Fred and Merrelyn Emery, attempt to help organization members envision an ideal future and then aim to achieve it. Such conferences are now used by practitioners such as Marvin Weisbord and Sandra Janoff, who help groups of more than sixty people, broken into smaller groups, analyze an organization's past, present, and preferred future. Managers (or a steering committee) record groups' ideas and integrate them into an action plan (Weisbord, 1987). Participative design, a methodology also developed by Fred and Merrelyn Emery, is a process for moving organizations from bureaucratic structures to democratic ones. Through a series of one-to two-day workshops, groups of approximately two dozen people redesign their jobs to meet six critical requirements (having decision-making freedom, opportunity to learn on the job, variety, mutual support and respect from peers and supervisors, a sense that one's work carries social meaning, and a career path for personal growth and increased knowledge and skills). Advocates of participative design maintain that by using this method, organizations can be redesigned in a matter of weeks rather than months (Canaba, 1995).

3. See Bob Filipczak, "Critical mass models," *Training* 32 (September 1995):38; Dick Axelrod, "Using the conference model for work redesign," *Journal for Quality and Participation* 16 (December 1993):58–61; and Axelrod, "Getting everyone involved: How one organization involved its employees, supervisors, and managers in redesigning the organization," *Journal of Applied Behavioral Science* 28 (December 1992):499–509.

Diffusion

It has already been established that work redesign efforts often fail to diffuse throughout organizations (Walton, 1975). This difficulty is rooted in much of the same problem that makes the redesign experience difficult to extend from the design team to the larger workforce: unless employees and managers are involved in the creation of the new work structures, they typically fail to understand and support them. This problem was most vividly apparent at Roseville. Unlike Santa Clara, a stand-alone division, the Roseville Surface Mount Center was nested within the walls of the larger manufacturing organization, in close contact with other units that were not undergoing redesign but upon which the center had to depend. As employees began venturing beyond the boundaries of the center, they encountered resistance from supervisors who did not know of, or who resisted the notion of, self-managing teams. Typically, these supervisors did not take employees seriously and insisted on dealing directly with supervisors, which left the center's employees angry and frustrated.

This study raises yet another dimension of diffusing a new organizational design. It suggests that organizations undertaking redesign must be able to exert sufficient control over their own strategic direction to coordinate the business strategy with the organizational redesign. This issue emerged in the Roseville Surface Mount Center, where the managers lacked both the formal sanction for a redesign and the authority to influence the company's personal computer strategy. Unlike the Santa Clara Division, which had control over its business charter, the Roseville Center's charter was under the direct control of the CPCD. Although Hendrickson obtained permission to conduct the redesign, she was unable to secure top managers' active support because they were focused on larger questions concerning the direction of HP's computer business. As one Roseville manager explained, managers at his level were not included in the discussions between the managers above them and had no control over the changes that were happening. After the center's redesign had been halted by top management's decision to consolidate manufacturing in France, it became clear to Roseville's managers that to succeed, the redesign had to be initiated at the same level at which the business strategy was made. Steve Tracy, the center's section manager, explained that redesigns must start from the top of an organization—which at HP is the level of the division—and that production, manufacturing, engineering, and marketing should be considered as components. That way, the center would have been tied into the division's business strategy and could have anticipated the necessary changes. He concluded that a redesign has to be high enough so that if the business shifts, the redesign effort can shift with it.

CONCLUSION

A growing number of companies are realizing that the flexibility they need to survive in fast-paced, turbulent environments resides in their employees. Economist Lester Thurow (1992:52) writes that in the century ahead, when natural resources, capital, and new product technologies will move rapidly around the world, "skilled people become the only sustainable competitive advantage." Successfully managing flexible manufacturing systems, he explains, will require "average workers with levels of education and skill that they have never had to have in the past" (52). Scholar Jeffrey Pfeffer (1994) points out that as new product and process technologies become easy to duplicate, employees and how they are managed are becoming an increasingly important competitive advantage. Management guru Peter Drucker maintains that employees' knowledge is not just another resource alongside the traditional factors of production—labor, land, and capital. Rather, it is *"the only meaningful resource today"* (1993:42).

The human quality that lies at the base of an organization's ability to adapt is peoples' capacity to learn. Companies such as Hewlett-Packard that are succeeding in this new environment know that investing in employees' ability to learn is not just a "nice thing to do." It is now a business imperative. Peter Senge writes in his best-selling book *The Fifth Discipline*, "The organizations that will truly excel in the future will be the organizations that discover how to tap people's commitment and capacity to learn at *all* levels of the organization" (1990:4). Learning must become continuous, and it must translate into tangible organizational change. As Michael Beer and Russell Eisenstat write, "Going through the realignment once is not enough. . . . Corporations will have to learn to reformulate strategy and realign their organizations continuously, if they are to survive in an increasingly turbulent environment. In short, corporations will have to become learning organizations capable of continuous adaptation" (1996: 598).

The question has been how to cultivate learning in companies that have grown around the needs of mass production. As we have seen, bringing about learning that leads to behavioral change is not always easy, especially when it requires exchanging entrenched and often cherished beliefs for new ones. This learning can occur only when employees feel a sense of security and fairness and are treated as assets rather than liabilities— values that HP's founders realized decades ago. Harnessing employees' knowledge and commitment also requires fundamental changes in organizations' structures. It may even require *"totally new organizations"* (Drucker, 1993:93). Organizations must dismantle their traditional, bureaucratic structures and the assumptions about power and authority that underlie them and replace them with flexible, decentralized structures in which employees have control over their work systems and can respond to customers' changing preferences by making decisions quickly. New incentives are also needed to encourage and support new behaviors. Once organizations become built around learning, change can become continuous.

In an effort to build such organizations, many companies have adopted rational, top-down strategies which, alone, are inadequate. The practice of TQM has been shown to bring about continuous although incremental change. But it has so far been unable to bring about more fundamental change because it is limited to working within an organization's existing business processes and its traditional, hierarchical structure. Other companies have embarked on reengineering. Though seductive because of fast returns, such reengineering efforts forget that, as Alan Webber, former editorial director of the *Harvard Business Review* says, "Knowledge only flows through the technology; it actually resides in people—in knowledge workers and the organizations they inhabit" (1993:24).

Building participative organizations that harness human potential and turn it into superior performance can be accomplished only through participation. In short, the means must fit the ends. In a reversal of Taylorism, which separated the design of work from its execution, employees must help lead organizational transformations. As Drucker points out, "The best way for people to learn how to be more productive is for them to teach. To obtain the improvement in productivity which the post-capitalist society now needs, the organization has to become both a learning and a teaching organization" (1993:92). Surviving in today's fast-paced, complex economic environment requires the full participation and support of employees, which can be achieved only by investing in their capacity to learn and by including them as partners in organizational change.

REFERENCES

Adler, Paul S. (1988). "Managing flexible automation." *California Management Review* 20 (1):35–56.

Allen, M., J. Brandemuehl, P. Gaarn, and D. Zell (1993). "Santa Clara Division: Becoming a customer-focused division through fast-cycle work redesign." Unpublished paper, Santa Clara Division.

Appelbaum, Eileen, and Rosemary Batt (1994). *The New American Workplace.* Ithaca: Cornell University Press.

Applebaum, Herbert A. (1981). *Royal Blue: The Culture of Construction Workers.* New York: Harper.

Auguston, Karen A. (1989). "Polaroid's journey to materials handling excellence—Part 1: Getting started." *Modern Materials Handling* 44 (July):60–63.

Bartlett, Christopher A., and Sumantra Ghoshal (1995). "Rebuilding behavioral context: Turn process reengineering into people rejuvenation." *Sloan Management Review* 37 (Fall):11–23.

Bashein, Barbara J., M. Lynne Markus, and Patricia Riley (1994). "Business reengineering: Preconditions for BPR success, and how to prevent failure." *Information Systems Management* 11:7–13.

Beer, Michael (1980). *Organizational Change and Development: A Systems View.* Santa Monica: Goodyear.

Beer, Michael, and Russell Eisenstat (1996). "Developing an organization capable of implementing strategy and learning." *Human Relations* 49 (5):597–619.

Beer, Michael, Russell Eisenstat, and B. Spector (1990). *The Critical Path to Corporate Renewal.* Boston: Harvard Business School Press.

Beer, Michael, and Elise Walton (1990). "Developing the competitive organization: Intervention and strategies." *American Psychologist* 45 (2):154–161.

Bogdan, Robert, and Sari Knopp Biklen (1982). *Qualitative Research for Education.* Boston: Allyn and Bacon.

163

Bolman, Lee G., and Terrence E. Deal (1984). *Modern Approaches to Understanding and Managing Organizations.* San Francisco: Jossey-Bass.

Braverman, Harry (1975). *Labor and Monopoly Capital: The Degradation of Work in the Twentieth Century.* New York: Monthly Review Press.

Byham, William C. (1988). *Zapp! The Lightning of Empowerment.* New York: Harmony Books.

Canaba, Steven (1995). "Participative design works, partially participative doesn't." *Journal for Quality and Participation* 18 (1) (January–February):10–19.

Chandler, Alfred D., Jr. (1977). *The Visible Hand: The Managerial Revolution in American Business.* Cambridge: The Belknap Press of Harvard University Press.

Cherns, Albert (1976). "The principles of sociotechnical design." *Human Relations* 29 (8):783–792.

—— (1987). "Principles of sociotechnical design revisited." *Human Relations* 40 (3):153–161.

Chinoy, Ely (1955). *Automobile Workers and the American Dream.* New York: Doubleday.

Chorn, Norman H. (1991). "Total quality management: panacea or pitfall?" *International Journal of Physical Distribution and Logistics Management* 11:31–35.

Conference Board (1991). *Employee Buy-In to Total Quality.* New York: Conference Board.

Cooper, Robin, and M. Lynne Markus (1995). "Human reengineering." *Sloan Management Review* 36 (Summer):39–50.

"Corporate objectives" (1989). Internal document #5957-2130. Hewlett-Packard Company, Corporate Offices, Palo Alto, Calif.

Dachler, H. Peter, and Bernhard Wilpert (1978). "Conceptual dimensions and boundaries of participation in organizations: A critical evaluation." *Administrative Science Quarterly* 23:1–39.

Davenport, Thomas H. (1993). "Need radical innovation and continuous improvement? Integrate process reengineering and TQM." *Planning Review* 21 (May–June):6–12.

—— (1995a). "The fad that forgot people." *Fast Company* 1(1):71–74.

—— (1995b). "Will participative makeovers of business processes succeed where reengineering failed?" *Planning Review* 23 (January–February): 24–29.

Davidson, William H., and Stanley M. Davis (1990). "Management and organization principles for the information economy." *Human Resource Management* 29 (Winter):365–383.

Davis, Louis E. (1957). "Toward a theory of job design." *Journal of Industrial Engineering* 8:1976–1993.

—— (1979). *Design of Jobs.* Santa Monica: Goodyear.

Davis, Louis E., and Albert B. Cherns, eds. (1975). *The Quality of Working Life*, Vol. 2. New York: Free Press.

Deming, W. Edwards (1986). *Out of the Crisis.* Cambridge: Massachusetts Institute of Technology, Center for Advanced Engineering Study.

Dertouzos, Michael, Richard Lester, Robert Solow, and the MIT Commission on Industrial Productivity (1989). *Made in America: Regaining the Productive Edge.* New York: HarperPerennial.

Drucker, Peter (1993) *The Post-Capitalist Society.* New York: HarperBusiness.

Economist (1995). "Re-engineering, with love." 336 (September 9):69–70.

Emery, Fred E. (1959). *Characteristics of Socio-Technical Systems.* Doc. 527. London: Tavistock Institute.

Filipczak, Bob (1995). "Critical mass models." *Training* 32 (September):38.

Fisher, Kim (1989). "Managing in the high-commitment workplace." *Organizational Dynamics* 17 (Winter):31–50.

Flamholtz, Eric (1995). "Back to 'basics': A holistic approach to organizational challenges." *Manage* 47 (July):13–15.

Flanigan, James (1996). "The great 'HP way' is Packard's legacy to American business." *Los Angeles Times* (March 17):D1.

Fukuyama, Francis (1995). *Trust: The Social Virtues and the Creation of Prosperity.* New York: Free Press.

Galliers, R. D., and B. S. H. Baker (1995). "An approach to business process reengineering: The contribution of socio-technical and soft OR concepts." *INFOR* 33 (November):263–278.

Garud, Raghu, and Kotha Suresh (1994). "Using the brain as a metaphor to model flexible production systems." *Academy of Management Review* 19 (October):671–698.

Garvin, David A. (1993). "Building a learning organization." *Harvard Business Review* 71 (July–August):78–91.

Geertz, Clifford (1973). "Thick description: Toward an interpretive theory of culture." In *The Interpretation of Cultures.* New York: Basic Books.

Goldhar, Joel D., Mariann Jelinek, and Theodore W. Schlie (1991). "Competitive advantage in manufacturing through information technology." *International Journal of Technology Management* 6:162–180.

Hackman, J. Richard, and G. Oldham (1980). *Work Redesign.* Reading, Mass.: Addison-Wesley.

Hackman, J. Richard, and Ruth Wageman (1995). "Total quality management: Empirical, conceptual, and practical issues." *Administrative Science Quarterly* 40 (June):309–342.

Haley, Michael (1985). "Effective business strategy: A Japanese example." *Human Systems Management* 5:191–205.

Hall, Gene, Jim Rosenthal, and Judy Wade (1993). "How to make reengineering really work." *Harvard Business Review* 71 (November–December): 119–131.

Hammer, Michael, and James Champy (1993). *Reengineering the Corporation.* New York: HarperBusiness.

Hardcastle, Alan (1994). "The Voices of Organizational Culture: An Ethnographic Study of Total Quality Management Implementation at Douglas Aircraft Company." Ph.D. diss., University of California at Los Angeles.

Harvard Business Reivew (1995). "Beyond total quality management and reengineering: Managing through processes" 73 (September–October):80–81.

Hayes, Robert H., Stephen C. Wheelwright, and Kim B. Clark (1988). *Dynamic Manufacturing: Creating the Learning Organization.* New York: Free Press.

Herbst, P. G. (1974). *Socio-Technical Design.* London: Tavistock.

Herrick, Neal (1990). *Joint Management and Employee Participation.* San Francisco: Jossey-Bass Publishers.

Hewlett-Packard Company (1995). *1995 Annual Report.* Palo Alto, Calif.

Hirschhorn, Larry (1984). *Beyond Mechanization: Work and Technology in a Postindustrial Age.* Cambridge: MIT Press.

Hitchcock, Darcy E., and Linda Lord (1992). "A convert's primer to sociotech." *Journal for Quality and Participation* 15 (June):46–57.

Hogan, Christine (1993). "How to get more out of videoconference meetings: A socio-technical approach, experience at Curtin University of Technology." *Training and Management Development Methods* 7 (1):5.01–5.16.

Hounshell, David (1984). *From the American System to Mass Production, 1800–1932.* Baltimore: John Hopkins University Press.

"HP Way" (1980). Internal document #5955-4709. Palo Alto, Calif.

Ichniowski, Casey, Kathryn Shaw, and Giovanna Prennushi (1993). "The effects of human resource management practice on productivity." Typescript. June.

Jaikumar, Ramchandran (1986). "Postindustrial manufacturing." *Harvard Business Review* 64 (November–December):69–76.

Johnson, Haynes (1994). *Divided We Fall.* New York: Norton.

Kanter, Rosabeth Moss (1993). "Mastering change." *Executive Excellence* 10 (April):11–12.

Katz, David, and Robert L. Kahn (1978). *The Social Psychology of Organizations.* New York: Wiley.

Kelly, John E. (1982). *Scientific Management, Job Redesign, and Work Performance.* London: Academic Press.

Ketchum, Lyman D. (1981). "How to start and sustain a work redesign program." *National Productivity Review* 1 (Winter):75–86.

Kilman, Ralph (1995). "A holistic program and critical success factors of corporate transformation." *European Management Journal* 13 (June):175–186.

Klein, Janice A. (1984). "Why supervisors resist employee involvement." *Harvard Business Review* 62 (September–October):87–95.

Kling, Jeffrey (1995). "High performance work systems and firm performance." *Monthly Labor Reviews* 118 (May):29–36.

Kotter, John, and James Heskett (1992). *Corporate Culture and Performance*. New York: Free Press.

Laabs, Jennifer J. (1993). "Successful restructurings depend on thinking big." *Personnel Journal* 72 (12):17.

Lathin, Drew (1995). "In the midst of the reengineering forest." *Journal for Quality and Participation* 18 (January–February):56–65.

Lawler, Edward E. III (1991). *High-Involvement Management*. San Francisco: Jossey-Bass.

—— (1994). "Total quality management and employee involvement: Are they compatible?" *Academy of Management Executive* 8 (1):68–76.

Lawler, Edward E. III, Susan Lalbers Mohrman, and Gerald E. Ledford, Jr. (1995). *Creating High Performance Organizations: Practices and Results of Employee Involvement and Total Quality Management in Fortune 1000 Companies*. San Francisco: Jossey-Bass.

Ledford, Gerald E., Jr., and Susan Albers Mohrman (1993). "Self-design for high involvement: A large-scale organizational change." *Human Relations* 46 (February):143–173.

Levine, David I. (1990). "Participation, productivity, and the firm's environment." *California Management Review* 32 (Summer):86–100.

—— (1995). *Reinventing the Workplace*. Washington, D.C.: Brookings.

Linden, Dana Wechsler, and Bruce Upbin (1996). "Top corporate performance of 1995. 'Boy Scouts on a rampage.'" *Forbes* 157 (January):66–70.

Macdonald, John (1995). "Together TQM and BPR are winners." *TQM Magazine* 7(3):21–25.

Macy, B., Izumi, Bliese, and Norton (1993). "Organizational change and work innovation: A meta-analysis of 131 North American field studies—1961–1991." In *Research in Organizational Change and Development*, Vol. 7.

Micklethwait, John, and Adrian Wooldridge (1996). *The Witch Doctors: Making Sense of the Management Gurus*. New York: Times Books.

Miles, Raymond E., and Howard R. Rosenberg (1982). "The human resources approach to management: Second generation issues." *Organizational Dynamics* 10 (Winter):26–41.

Mohrman, Susan A., and Allan M. Mohrman, Jr. (1989). *Organizing for the Future*. San Francisco: Jossey-Bass.

Mohrman, Susan A., Ramkrishnan V. Tenkasi, Edward E. Lawler III, and Gerald E. Ledford, Jr. (1995). "Total quality management: Practices and outcomes in the largest US firms." *Employee Relations* 17 (3):26–41.

Nora, John J., C. Raymond Rogers, and Robert J. Stramy (1986). *Transforming the Workplace*. Princeton: Princeton Research Press.

Ouchi, William G. (1981). *Theory Z.* Reading, Mass.: Addison-Wesley.

Packard, David (1974). Unpublished transcript of meeting between David Packard and Bay Area division managers, February 11.

—— (1995). *The HP Way.* New York: HarperCollins.

Pascale, Richard T., and Anthony G. Athos (1981). *The Art of Japanese Management.* New York: Simon & Schuster.

Pasmore, William A., and K. Gurley (1991). "Enhancing R&D across functional areas." In Ralph Kilmann and Ines Kilmann, eds., *Making Organizations Competitive.* San Francisco: Jossey-Bass.

Pasmore, William A., and John J. Sherwood (1992). "Some real life results of sociotechnical systems design." Undocumented memo. San Francisco: Organization Consultants, Inc.

Pava, Calvin H. (1983). *Managing New Office Technology.* New York: Free Press.

Peters, Thomas J., and Robert H. Waterman (1982). *In Search of Excellence: Lessons from America's Best Run Companies.* New York: Harper & Row.

Pfeffer, Jeffrey (1994). *Competitive Advantage through People.* Boston: Harvard Business School Press.

Pine, Joseph B. II (1993). *Mass Customization.* Boston: Harvard Business School Press.

Powers, Jack E. (1972). "Job enrichment—how one company overcame the obstacles." *Personnel* 49 (3):19–22.

Purser, Ronald E. (1991). "Redesigning the knowledge-based product development organization: A case study of sociotechnical systems change." *Technovation* 11(7):403–416.

Purser, Ronald E., and William A. Pasmore (1990). "Designing effective knowledge utilization systems in R&D: A case study of nonroutine sociotechnical systems change." In Michael W. Lawless and Luiz R. Gomez-Mejia, eds., *Strategic Management in High Technology Firms.* Greenwich: Jai Press.

Reese, Rick (1995). "Redesigning for dial tone: A socio-technical systems case study." *Organizational Dynamics* 24 (Autumn):80–90.

Rehder, Robert, Narta Smith, and Katherine Burr (1989). "A salute to the sun: Crosscultural organisational adaptation and change." *Leadership and Organization Development Journal* 10 (4):17–27.

Rice, Albert K. (1958). *Productivity and Social Organizations: The Ahmedabad Experiment.* London: Tavistock.

Rohlen, Thomas P. (1974). *For Harmony and Strength: Japanese White Collar Organization, an Anthropolgical Perspective.* Berkeley: University of California Press.

Roy, D. (1952). "Quota restriction and goldbricking in a machine shop." *American Journal of Sociology* 57:427–442.

Rummler, Geary A., and Alan P. Brache (1990). *Process Management: Managing the White Space on the Organization Chart*. San Francisco: Jossey-Bass.

Sabel, Charles F. (1993). "Studied trust: Building new forms of cooperation in a volatile economy." *Human Relations* 46 (September):1133–1170.

Savage, Charles H., and George F. F. Lombard (1986). *Sons of the Machine: Case Studies of Social Change in the Workplace*. Cambridge: MIT Press.

Scarpa, James (1991). "McDonald's menu mission." *Restaurant Business* (July 1):117. In Pine (1993).

Schaffer, Robert H. (1988). *The Breakthrough Strategy; Using Short-Term Success to Build the High Performance Organization*. Cambridge: Ballinger.

Schein, Edgar H. (1968). "Organizational socialization and the profession of management." *Industrial Management Review* 9:1–15.

—— (1989). *Organizational Culture and Leadership*. Sn Francisco: Jossey-Bass.

Schoenberger, Karl (1992). "Japan's L.A. consul general exudes optimism." *Los Angeles Times (July* 13):D3.

Senge, Peter M. (1990). *The Fifth Discipline: The Art and Practice of the Learning Organization*. New York: Doubleday Currency.

Sheridan, John H. (1993). "Agile manufacturing: Stepping beyond lean production." *Industry Week* 242 (April 19):30–46.

—— (1995). "Which path to follow?" *Industry Week* 244 (July 3):41–45.

Sherwood, John J. (1988). "Creating work cultures with competitive advantage." *Organizational Dynamics* 16 (Winter 1988):5–27.

Special Task Force to the Secretary of Health, Education, and Welfare (1973). *Work in America*. Cambridge, Mass: N.p.

Spira, Joel S., and Joseph B. II Pine (1993). "Mass customization." *Chief Executive* 83 (March):26–29.

Starbuck, William H., and John M. Dutton (1973). "Designing adaptive organizations." *Journal of Business Policy* 3 (4):21–28.

Taylor, F. C., P. W. Gustavson, and W. S. Carter (1986). "Integrating the social and technical systems of organizations." In Donald D. Davis, ed., *Managing Technological Innovation*. San Francisco: Jossey Bass.

Taylor, Frederick Winslow (1919). *Shop Management*. New York: Harper & Brothers.

—— (1967). *The Principles of Scientific Management*. New York: Harper & Brothers.

Taylor, James C., and David F. Felton (1993). *Performance by Design*. New York: Prentice-Hall.

Teng, James T. C., Varun Grover, and Kirk D. Fiedler (1994). "Business process reengineering: Charting a strategic path for the information age." *California Management Review* 36 (3):9–31.

Teresko, John (1994). "Mass customization or mass confusstion?" *Industry Week* 243 (June 20):45–48.

Thurow, Lester C. (1992). *Head to Head.* New York: William Morrow.

—— (1995a). "Thriving in turbulent times." *Executive Excellence* 12 (November):3–4.

—— (1995b). "Regaining our competitiveness." *Executive Excellence* 8 (June):11–12.

Trist, Eric L. (1976). "Critique of scientific management in terms of sociotechnical theory." In M. Weir, ed., *Job Satisfaction.* London: Fontana.

—— (1981). "The evolution of socio-technical systems." Occasional Paper No. 2. In Andrew Van de Ven and Willam Joyce, *Perspectives on Organizational Design and Behaviour.* New York: Wiley.

Trist, Eric L., and Kenneth Bamforth (1951). "Some social and psychological consequences of the longwall method of coal getting." *Human Relations* 4:3–39.

Trist, Eric L., G. Higgin, H. Murray, and A. B. Pollock (1963). *Organizational Choice.* London: Tavistock.

Van Maanen, John (1977). "Experiencing organizations." In John Van Maanen, ed., *Organizational Careers: Some New Perspectives.* New York: Wiley.

von Bertalanffy, Ludwig (1950). "The theory of open systems in physics and biology." *Science* 3:23–29.

von Werssowetz, Richard, and Michael Beer (1982). "Human resources at Hewlett-Packard." HBS Case Services, No. 482-125. Boston: Harvard Business School.

Walker, Charles R., and Robert H. Guest (1952). *The Man on the Assembly Line.* Cambridge: Harvard University Press.

Wall Street Journal (1991). "A 1990 reorganization at Hewlett-Packard already is paying off." July 22: Al(W), Al(E), col. 6.

Walton, Richard E. (1972). "How to counter alienation in the plant." *Harvard Business Review* 50 (6):70–81.

—— (1975). "The diffusion of new work structures: Explaining why success didn't take." *Organizational Dynamics* 3 (Winter):2–22.

—— (1977). "Successful strategies for diffusing work innovations." *Journal of Contemporary Business* 6 (Spring):1–22.

—— (1985). "From control to commitment in the workplace." *Harvard Business Review* 63 (March–April):76–84.

—— (1987). *Innovating to Compete: Lessons for Diffusing and Managing Change in the Workplace.* San Francisco: Jossey-Bass.

Walton, Richard E., and Gerald I. Susman (1987). "People policies for the new machines." *Harvard Business Review* 65 (March–April):98–106.

Wax, Rosalie H. (1971). *Doing Fieldwork: Warning and Advice.* Chicago: University of Chicago Press.

Webber, Alan M. (1993). "What's so new about the new economy?" *Harvard Business Review* 71 (January–February):24–32+.

Weisbord, Marvin R. (1987). *Productive Workplaces: Organizing and Managing for Dignity, Meaning, and Community.* San Francisco: Jossey-Bass.

Whitsett, David A. (1975a). "Where are your unenriched jobs?" *Harvard Business Review* 53 (January–February): 74–80.

—— (1975b). "Making sense of management theories." *Personnel* 52 (3):44–52.

Whyte, William Foote (1961). *Men at Work.* Homewood, Ill: Dorsey Press.

Wilms, Wellford W. (1996). *Restoring Prosperity.* New York: Random House.

Womack, James P. (1995). Review of *The Reengineering Revolution: A Handbook* and *The Mandate for a New Leadership. Sloan Management Review* 36 (Summer):99–100.

Womack, James P., Daniel T. Jones, and Daniel D. Roos (1990). *The Machine That Changed the World.* New York: Rawson Associates.

Yorks, Lyle (1976). *A Radical Approach to Job Enrichment.* New York: AMACOM.

Yorks, Lyle, and David Whitsett (1989). *Scenarios of Change: Advocacy and the Diffusion of Job Redesign in Organizations.* New York: Praeger.

Zager, Robert, and Michael Rosow, eds. (1982). *The Innovation Organization: Productivity Programs in Action.* New York: Pergamon Press.

Zell, Deone, Harold Levine, and Wellford Wilms (1992). "The impact of the work innovation network on the diffusion of work redesign at Hewlett-Packard." Unpublished paper, University of California at Los Angeles.

INDEX

alignment, organizational, 3, 5, 135–140, 154. *See also entries for specific sites*
Allen, Mark, 101, 118
Aluminum Company of Canada, 29
Apple Computer, 114
assembly line. *See* mass production
AT&T, 16, 29
automobile industry, Japan and, 10

Baldridge National Quality Award, 20
Barclays Bank, 11
Bartlett, Christopher, 23
Beer, Michael, 160
BPR. *See* Business Process Reengineering
Brandemuehl, Jenny, 89, 93, 98, 102, 109, 112, 116–117, 130–131, 151, 157
Bull's-Eye model, 137. *See also* Sociotechnical Systems redesign; *entries for individual sites*
Business Process Reengineering (BPR), 4, 16, 136, 148 , 154, 161
definition of, 21–22

drawbacks and demise of, 23
need for, 14
need for reform of, 23–24
popularity of, 22–23
See also entries for individual sites

Caterpillar Inc., 11
Champion Paper, 109
Champy, James, 22
changing by design
broadening perspectives, 146–148
complexity of sharing power in, 143–146
diffusing redesign, 159
harnessing human potential, 141–161
institutionalizing new behaviors, 152
learning by design, 146–150
lengthiness of, 155–157
need for leadership in, 155
obtaining commitment in, 148–149
overcoming cultural obstacles to change, 149–150
overcoming resistance to change, 151–152

173

changing by design (cont.)
  prerequisites to, 141–142
  redesigning organizations as sys-
    tems, 135–140
  remaining obstacles to, 154–160
  transferring learning, 157–158
  translating learning into new be-
    haviors, 150
  translating new behaviors into or-
    ganizational performance, 152–
    154
Chase Manhattan Bank, 11
Cherns, Albert, 26
Citibank, 30
competition:
  changing nature of, 10–11
  "little tigers" and, 10
computer-aided design and manufac-
    turing, 11
computer-integrated manufacturing,
    13
craft production, 7
CSC Index, 23
culture:
  imperviousness of, 141
  as obstacle to change, 17–18,
    149–150
  See also entries for indiviual sites
Cummins Engine, 29, 30
customers, changing preferences of,
    12

Davenport, Thomas, 23, 24, 148
Davis, Louis, 26
Davis, Stan, 13
Deming, W. Edwards, 20, 21
diffusion. See changing by design
Digital Equipment, 29, 51, 55
Drucker, Peter, 15, 160–161
DuPont, 11

Early, Dennis, 51–52, 82, 84–86,
    153, 156
Eastern Sales Region, HP, 88

Eastern Sales Support Office, HP,
    109
Eisenstat, Russell, 160
electronics industry, Japan and, 10
Emery, Fred, 26, 158
Emery, Merrelyn, 158
employees:
  as assets, 160
  capacity to learn, 3
  expanded roles, 14
  ignored in reengineering, 23
  as leaders of transformational ef-
    forts, 5, 161
  need for skilled and committed, 14
    15, 135
  need to compensate, 14
  as partners in organizational
    change, 5, 161
employment security, 160. See also
  changing by design; entries for
  individual sites
empowerment, 148
  as business imperative, 143
  lack of, despite popularity, 18
  willingness to accept, 145–156
  See also entries for individual sites
ethnography. See research methods

Factory of the Future, 40, 51, 58
fairness, 160; as prerequisite to
    change, 141–142
Fifth Discipline, The (Peter Senge),
    160
flexible manufacturing, 13
focus groups. See research methods
Ford, Henry, 7, 8
Ford Motor Company, 7
future-search conferences. See Socio-
    technical Systems redesign

gainsharing, 16
General Electric, 16, 30
General Foods, 29, 157
General Motors, 29

Ghoshall, Sumantra, 23
Global Positioning System (GPS), 97
Guest, Robert, 9

H. J. Heinz, 29
Hackman, J. Richard, 21
Hammer, Michael, 22
Hendrickson, Kathy, 50–54, 58–63,
    65–66, 68–71, 73, 75, 80–81,
    83–84, 86, 143–145, 155–157,
    159
Herzberg, Frederick, 15
Hewlett, William, 35, 36, 39, 40,
    141
Hewlett-Packard Company (HP):
    culture of, 36–40, 123, 146
    employment security at, 142
    flexible hours at, 39
    foundation and growth of, 35
    structure of, 35–36
    teamwork at, 37
    See also HP Way
high-performance organization, 136
Hoechst, 11
Honeywell, 30
HP Labs, 122, 142
HP Way, 36, 141
    compatibility with SCD's new
        values, 94
    compatibility with STS redesign,
        135
    core belief behind, 136, 141–142
    employment security of, 39
    erosion of, at Roseville, 59–60
    "family feeling" of, 39–40
    management by objectives (MBO)
        and by walking around
        (MBWA), 38
    in practice, 38–40
    values and objectives of, 36–38
Hughes Aircraft, 87

IBM, 117
Inland Steel, 29

interviews. *See* research methods
Ishikawa, Kaoru, 20, 21

Janoff, Sandra, 158
Job Diagnostic Survey (Hackman
    and Oldham), 59
job enrichment, 15
Johnson and Johnson, 29
Juran, Joseph, 20, 21

Ketchum, Lyman, 157
Komatsu, 11

leadership, need for in redesign,
    154–155
learning:
    investing in employees' capacity
        for, 4, 153–154
    through redesign, 146–148
    translating into new behavior,
        135–136
    transferring to "critical mass" of
        employees, 157–158
learning organization, 160

Made in America (Dertouzos et al.),
    15–17
mass customization, 4
    adoption of, by different indus-
        tries, 13–14
    goal of, 13
    implications of, 14
    replacing culture of, 17
    self-managing teams and, 14
mass production, 4, 148, 160
    assembly line as hallmark of, 7
    complacency following, 10
    culture of, 3
    deleterious effects of, 9
    as precursor to hierarchical organi-
        zations, 8–9
    scientific management and, 8
    success of, 9–10, 15
McDonald's, 14

McDonnell Douglas, 87
Mead, 29
MIT Commission on Industrial Productivity, 17
Motorola, 30

NEC, 55
Neil, Marty, 39, 87–92, 94–96, 98, 102–105, 108–109, 112, 114, 116, 118, 121–123, 129–131, 138–139, 143–144, 146–147, 151, 155–158
Northern Telecom, 117

open system, 25
organizational redesign. *See* Sociotechnical Systems redesign
organizations as systems, 3–5, 16, 136

Packard, David, 35–36, 39–40, 141
parallel structures, 17
participant-observation. *See* research methods
participative design. *See* Sociotechnical Systems redesign
participative management, new need for, 15
Pfeffer, Jeffrey, 160
Pierce, Terry, 51–52, 70, 72
Pine, Joseph, II, 13
PPG Industries, 29
problem-solving teams, 17
process technology vs. product technology, 11
Proctor & Gamble, 29–30
profit sharing, 3

Qualcomm project (first Sync product), 128–129
quality circles, 3, 16–17
Quality of Work Life, 15
quality revolution, SCD and, 87

R&D process, standardization of, 101–102, 118, 145
rapid response. *See* mass customization
reengineering. *See* Business Process Reengineering
research methods, 4
confidentiality and anonymity, 44
critical incidents, 45
database development, 45
ethnography, 35, 42
focus groups, 43, 45–47
interviews, 42–43, 46
participant-observation, 42–44
"shadowing," 44–45
social analyses, 45
survey research, 43, 45–47
Rockwell, 29
Roseville Surface Mount Center:
adaptability, 86, 153
adoption of, by Roseville Network Division (RND), 80–81, 83
alignment, 152
benchmarking, 51, 55
Bull's-Eye model, 61–62
business analysis, 55–56, 60, 86, 147, 153
California Personal Computer Division (CPCD) and, 49, 159
change in charter, 81
commitment at, 148
communication, 58
competitiveness of, 50
counsels (groups), 75
culture of, 58–60, 149
customers, 55, 73, 147
decision making, 150
design team, 53
Design Week, 60–71
diffusion at, 78–80, 159
downsizing, 60, 81–83, 142
employment security, 59, 142
empowerment, 71, 76–80, 85, 145, 148, 150

Roseville Surface Mount Center (*cont.*)
 engineers, 67, 79, 106, 145
 ethnic diversity, 68, 74–75, 142
 evaluation system, 69, 76, 82, 137,
  143, 152
 goal of, 52
 Green Team, 83–84
 high-performance organization
  simulation, 54, 73, 77
 Hoshin of, 52
 HP Way, 59–60, 63
 institutionalizing new behaviors,
  152
 just-in-time production, 55–56
 leadership at, 155
 learning organization, 64, 86, 156
 learning through redesign, 146–
  149, 153
 lengthiness of redesign, 84–85,
  156–157
 lessons from, 135–136
 level of redesign, 159
 maintenance technicians, 67–68
 management at, 60, 67
 meaning of "team," 66, 149
 New Product and Process Introduction (NPPI) Counsel, 83
 orientation, 69
 ownership, 148
 pace of change, 50, 84, 156
 performance improvement of, 80,
  83–84, 85–86, 152–153
 Personal Computer Group, 50
 power sharing, 143–145
 prerequisites to behavioral change,
  142
 prestige at, 65
 Process Improvement Teams
  (PITs), 56
 production process, 49–50
 production relationship map, 56
 proposal for redesign, 71–72
 ranking. *See subentry*: evaluation
  system

 redefining roles, 67–68, 75
 redesigning organizations as systems, 135, 137
 relocation from Sunnyvale, 50
 resistance to change, 74, 78–80
 responsiveness of, 55
 reward system, 69, 76, 137
 selection system, 69, 82
 self-managing teams, 52, 66, 82,
  137, 144, 149–150, 152
 social analysis, 58–60, 153
 stakeholders, 56
 statistical process control (SPC),
  56, 64–65, 67, 137, 146
 Statistical Process Control Counsel, 83
 steering committee, 52–53
 STS redesign, 73
 Summer School, 72–75, 84,
  157
 supervisors, 67, 79, 82, 137
 teamwork, 70–71, 75–76, 142,
  149
 technical analysis, 56–58, 60, 86,
  136, 153
 technology at, 49, 53, 55
 temporary employees, 68–69, 71
 threat of consolidation, 53–54
 training, 69, 72, 82
 transferring learning to employees,
  157–158
 translating learning into new behavior, 150
 translating new behaviors into organizational performance, 153
 tribal knowledge, 58
 variances, 58, 60, 64–65, 152
 vision for, 52–53, 62–64

Santa Clara Division (SCD):
 accountability, 99, 111, 117, 122,
  126–127, 139–140, 146, 149–
  150, 152
 adaptability of, 154

Santa Clara Division (SCD) (*cont.*)
  alignment, 96, 98, 102–103, 109, 152
  benchmarking, 109
  Bull's-Eye model, 110
  business analysis and strategy, 88, 89, 138, 139, 147
  businesses of, 90–91, 139
  Business Strategy Review (BSR), 89
  Cold War and, 87
  commitment at, 148–149
  culture of, 94, 101, 107, 131–132, 139–140, 147
  customer focus, 105–107, 111, 115, 118, 123–124, 127–128, 130, 139–140, 145, 151, 143
  customers, 87, 89, 138
  customer segment managers (CSMs), 92
  customer segments, 91, 139
  decision making, 89–92, 96, 122, 131, 139
  defense cutbacks and, 87
  Design-Build-Sell-Support (DBSS), 105
  diffusion at, 159
  downsizing, 88, 121, 142
  Electronic Instruments Group, 88
  employment security, 118, 142
  empowerment, 91, 103–104, 111–112, 131, 139, 143, 149, 155
  environment surrounding, 87, 102
  evaluation system, 111, 116–117, 122, 140, 152, 156
  flexibility, 112, 121
  free market concept, 112–113, 117, 122, 130, 139, 152
  goal of, 138
  growth, 90, 129, 154
  Hoshins of, 95–96
  HP Way, 111, 113, 118, 120
  incentive system, 96, 112

  institutionalizing new behaviors, 152
  leadership at, 104, 108–109, 155
  learning through redesign, 127–128, 130–131, 146–150
  lengthiness of redesign, 116, 156–157
  lessons from, 135–136
  level of redesign, 159
  macro-level redesign, 88–94
  management at, 103–104
  market choice process, 91, 93
  matrix structure, 91, 109
  micro-level redesign, 88, 98–115
  morale at, 120–121
  New Product and Process Services (NPPS) organization, 92, 139
  New Product Development (NPD) team, 88, 98, 139
  new product development process at, 89, 91–94, 96, 109, 118, 139
  next-bench syndrome of, 90
  order fulfillment (manufacturing) process, 91–92, 139
  overcoming resistance to change, 151
  ownership at, 99, 113, 130, 151
  pay system, 111, 117, 156
  performance improvement of, 129–131, 154
  power sharing at, 103–104, 131, 143–145, 155
  Precision Motion Control (PMC) customer segment, 91
  prerequisites to behavioral change and, 142
  product choice process, 91
  products, 87, 127–128
  program leader concept, 103–104, 112–113
  project reviews (postpartums), 98, 118, 140

Santa Clara Division (SCD) (*cont.*)
proposal for redesign, 102, 112–115
quality revolution, 87
R&D process, 101–102
redesigning organizations as systems, 135, 137, 138, 139
reengineering, 98–102, 139, 148
resistance to change, 105–107, 114, 118, 121–122, 145, 149–151
responsiveness of, 131, 140
restructuring, 92, 94, 120, 131, 145
Return-On-Investment (ROI), 89
SDBS team, 124–128, 154
self-managing teams, 105, 116–117, 124–126, 130, 150–151, 154
Sell-Design-Build-Support (SDBS), 96, 105–106, 117, 124, 129, 154
6X project review, 98–99
skepticism about redesign, 105, 120–121, 131
skit to ease anxiety, 118–120
social analysis, 89, 111–112, 138, 146, 156
standardizing creativity, 145
steering committee, 103–104
strategic management retreat, 103–104
strengths and weaknesses, 89
structure of, 90–91, 94, 105, 138–139
STS redesign, 88, 110–111
Synchronization (Sync) business at, 96–98, 105, 119–120, 124, 130
team-based systems, 109, 114–115, 117, 140
teams and teamwork, 112, 113–114, 126, 149
technical analysis, 91, 109–110, 138

Timing Solutions for Communications (TSC) customer segment, 91, 116
training, 96, 111, 114, 124, 156
transferring learning to employees, 158
transition team, 88, 98, 139
translating learning into new behavior, 150
translating new behaviors into organizational performance, 154
values of, 88, 94–95
SCD. *See* Santa Clara Division
scientific management. *See* mass production
Seagate, 117
security. *See* employment security
self-managing teams, 16, 17
mass customization and, 14
survival rates of, 18
See also entries under individual sites
Senge, Peter, 160
Shell Oil, 29, 30
Sherwin-Williams, 29
Shultz, Bob, 88
SmartClock, 97, 129, 154
Sociotechnical Systems (STS) redesign, 24
and alignment, 154
benchmarking, 28
Bull's-Eye model of, 61–62, 110
business analysis, 26–28
culture analysis, 28
compared with TQM and BPR, 154
consultants, 28
as continuous process, 86, 157
customer requirements, 28
design team, 26
diffusion of, 159
and empowerment, 154
and future-search conferences, 158

Sociotechnical Systems (STS) (*cont.*)
  at Hewlett-Packard, 40
  HP Way's compatibility with, 51,
    135
  large-group methodologies and,
    158
  as learning tool, 4, 146–148
  lengthiness of, 154–157
  mission and values, 28
  and strategic direction, 159
  in nonlinear environments, 30
  in Norway and Sweden, 25
  origin of, 25
  participative redesign and, 158
  policies and practices in, 28
  principles and process of, 26–28
  proposal in, 28
  at Roseville, 40–41, 73
  at Saab, 26
  at Santa Clara, 41, 88, 110–111
  skepticism about, 110
  social analysis, 26
  sponsorship of, 26
  stakeholders in, 26
  steering committee, 26
  and strategic direction, 159
  technical analysis, 26–28
  tenets of, 25, 136
  theory behind, 25
  use of, 29–30
  at Volvo, 26
steel industry, Japan and, 10
STS redesign. *See* Sociotechnical Systems redesign
survey research. *See* research
  methods
systems, organizations as, 16, 135

Tavistock Institute, 25
Taylor, Frederick Winslow, 8
Taylorism, 23, 161

Tecktronix, 29
Thirumale, Murli, 96–97, 103–104,
  107–108, 120, 122, 128–129,
  143, 147
Thurow, Lester, 15, 160
time-based competition. *See* mass
  customization
Toffler, Alvin, 13
Total Quality Management (TQM),
  4, 16, 22, 136, 154, 161
  drawbacks of, 21
  implementation of, 20
  origin of, 19
  popularity of, 20–21
  practice of, 20
Toyota, 14
Tracy, Steve, 51, 59–60, 65, 67, 72,
  79–81, 83, 85–86, 142–144,
  155, 159
trade deficit, 10
Trist, Eric, 25, 26
trust, as prerequisite to change, 141–
  142
TRW, 29–30

UCLA research team, 59, 111, 156
unions, lack of at HP, 142

Volvo, 29, 30

Wageman, Ruth, 21
Walker, Charles, 9
Webber, Alan, 161
Weisbord, Marvin, 159
Winby, Stu, 40
Work in America (Special Task
  Force), 9, 29
workforce. *See* employees
World War II, 9–10

*Zapp! The Lightning of Empower-
  ment* (William Byham), 75–76